TTIC PRESS

DUBLIN BELLES

First published in 1988 by
Attic Press,
44 East Essex Street,
Dublin 2.

Johnston, Máirín, 1931-
    Dublin belles: conversations with Dublin women.
    1. Dublin. Social life, **1905-1988**.
    Biographies. Collections
    I. Title
    941.8'35082'0922
    ISBN 0-946211-50-7
    ISBN 0-946211-49-3 Pbk

Cover Design: Design II.
Typesetting: Phototype-Set Ltd., Dublin.
Printing: Leinster Leader, Naas.

Photographs of *Nuala O'Faolain* and *Pauline Cummins* supplied by courtesy of *The Irish Times*.

Acknowledgements

    I would like to express my sincere thanks to all of the women in *Dublin Belles* who very generously gave of their time to speak to me about their memories and experiences of growing up in Dublin. Some of the women I already knew, others I had the pleasure of meeting for the first time. I hope they all found the interviews as enjoyable as I did.
    I would also like to thank Attic Press for asking me to take part in this Millennium project and for all the help and support given to me while carrying it out.

Máirín Johnston.

Born in 1931, Máirín Johnston grew up in the heart of the Liberties, where her family on her mother's side had lived since 1850 and on her father's side since 1680. She attended St Brigid's National School, the Coombe, until she was 14 years of age. Until her marriage in 1952, she worked in various shirt factories and in Jacob's Biscuit Factory. Her main interests are music, politics, literature, the women's movement and social history. She is the mother of two girls and two boys. In 1983 her book, AROUND THE BANKS OF PIMLICO, was published. It immediately reached the bestsellers list and remained there for more than two months. She is currently researching her next publication.

DEDICATION

To the memory of my mother, a wonderful Dublin belle, who was born 100 years ago in 1888.

CONTENTS

AnCO*	National Training Agency
ARP	Air Raid Precautions
ATS	Auxiliary Training Services
CIE	Authority for the Provision of Public Transport
ESB	Electricity Supply Board
Glimmerman	Gas Company Inspector during the war whose job was to check on customers and to cut off the gas if it was being used during unauthorised hours
IDA	Industrial Development Authority
KLEAR	Kilbarrack Local Education for Adult Renewal
LDF	Local Defence Forces
LSF	Local Security Forces
RTE	National Broadcasting Station
SPUC	Society for the Protection of the Unborn
UCD	University College Dublin
YEA*	Youth Employment Agency

AnCO and the YEA are now part of FÁS, The Training and Employment Authority.

Introduction

What do Dublin women think about their city? Are they concerned about what has happened to their long established communities, to their Georgian heritage, to their roadways, to the quality of life in the city? To find out the answers to these questions I was commissioned by Attic Press to interview on tape a representative cross section of women with a view to publishing their opinions, their memories, their experiences and their vision of Dublin as we head into the twenty first century.

The result is this warm, witty and informative collection of interviews with twenty four Dublin women of all ages and religions, with different social backgrounds and experiences. It covers a period of seventy eight years, from 1910 to 1988 and is a valuable contribution to the Dublin Millennium celebrations.

It is also a unique social history of Dublin, recording as it does the roles women have played and are continuing to play in the day to day life of the city. Some of the women are very well known, nationally and internationally. Others are known only within their own areas. Whatever they happen to be engaged in the women are making history. Each woman's recollection of her time and place adds an important dimension to the overall collection.

Almost eight decades of the city's history are recorded in the interviews. During these decades many dramatic changes took place of a social and political character, not least the establishment of the State. Although the oldest women were only small children when the Easter Rising took place they have vivid memories of some of the happenings at the time.

This is not a book about the past although there are references go leor to the ' rare oul' times. ' Neither is it a dry history full of dates and battles. It is humorous and informative and forward looking. There are many amusing anecdotes alongside the deeply committed concern the women have for the city's future and the quality of life of its people. The women are not passive observers of events. Each one of them has made a significant contribution to some aspect of Dublin life and continues to do so. It is very apparent how much they love their city and feel strongly that it has a unique quality which is worth striving to preserve.

Many of them couldn't live anywhere else. Some tried but came back.

A few interesting questions cropped up in the course of the interviews. What, for instance, constitutes a real Dub? How many generations of a family must have lived in Dublin before a claim can be made? Do real Dubs only come from certain areas of the city such as the Liberties, Ringsend or Summerhill?

After reading Dublin Belles the answers should be clear. Every part of the city is represented, every social stratum and all religions. Each has very definite views on their native city and how it should be run.

All those whose memories go back furthest, to the 1950s and beyond, express the viewpoint that although there is a great deal of poverty around now, it is nothing like the poverty years ago when ragged, barefoot children could be seen everywhere.

The descriptions of student life in the 1950s and '60s, while hilarious to read about, nevertheless vividly convey the repressive nature of society then and the fear of authority which this repression generated in everyone.

How have Dubliners of minority religions felt about their city? What way were they treated by their Catholic neighbours? Why have their numbers decreased? The answers are there with some very moving comments.

Inevitably there is a certain amount of nostalgia expressed for those aspects of Dublin's past which are now but pleasant memories — clear air, clear water and clear roads. The living city that was safe to walk through at night, the enjoyment of window shopping on fine evenings, the childrens' street games played on safe roads, the theatre going that was a normal social pastime, when there were beautiful theatres to go to, all are fondly remembered.

Máirín Johnston, 1988.

Tina Byrne

My mother came from Coombe Street and my da from Bride Street. I was born in the Coombe Hospital and we lived in Fatima Mansions where I still live. I'm very involved in the community.

There always seemed to be a buzz around Fatima whether it was just the kids running around or the people coming from the pubs in the evenings, or the singing that went on in the corners. On New Year's Eve, all the people would be out on the square holding hands around the line poles.

As kids we'd a brilliant time. The caretakers were very strict in the beginning, you couldn't play in the flats, so we'd play outside. We'd go over to the canal, when it was still there, and bring our milk bottles and fishing rods and collect pinkeens, or we'd go over to the far side of the canal and collect blackberries. Then straight on down to Ghost Town, where we weren't allowed, at the very end of the canal.

I don't know what was there before that. But it was an old town and it became really decayed on the Grand Canal banks. There were old houses and old buildings and we used to have a fabulous time. It was very dangerous and I remember getting a hiding when my mother found out because, number one, you weren't supposed to cross the road and, two, you weren't to go across to the canal and, three, you especially weren't supposed to go to Ghost Town. But we always went back for more.

Fatima was brilliant. You'd have the old down and outs coming around and singing and Ma would give me the tuppence or threepence or whatever to throw over the balcony to them. It was just wonderful.

Our local school was Basin Lane, James's Street and that's where my own child is going now. We had a really strict nun there at the time. If you weren't allowed to mix with the crowd from Fatima you went to Loreto.

The old Basin Lane was there when I started school. The Iron Bridge was still there at that stage and it was terrible having to cross it on a frosty morning. You were in danger of breaking your neck. But we didn't use it often because the fellas swam in the canal in the summer time, then we'd put planks across it and run

over without having to go over the bridge. If we were on the mitch from school we could hide in the old Basin.

A neighbour was telling a story the other day about his brother who found a hand in the Basin. There were headlines all over the paper, 'THIS IS THE HAND THAT SHOOK JAMES'S STREET....' It was actually a skeleton hand that he'd found and they had great fun hiding it up the sleeve of their coat offering it to people to shake hands.

I don't know if they ever found out who owned the hand or how long it had been there. The Basin is still there. It's just a wall with a patch of grass now. It is a little piece of history, I suppose, but how many people know about it?

I remember the canal, it was dirty, filthy in fact, and the swans. It was a big treat when the swans came up and down and we'd get our bread and Da would take us across to feed them. I have such vivid memories of that. I also have images of the other extreme when it was full of prams and weeds all round the edges, and dead animals — you always had that.

Another great pastime for the fellas was catching rats out of the canal. It's not really funny. They'd throw them around the wires outside the flats and you'd have a display of rats along the wires which didn't do much to improve the image of the area at all.

The canal locks are still there. A little lad from Fatima lost his life there tragically. He got trapped underneath the lock and couldn't get back up. I couldn't swim, still can't, although I love the water. I just don't seem to be able to float on the stuff.

We used to go up there, especially in the summer, and the fellas would have races across and we'd be sitting on the bridge. There was great skit at the end of it, we had such laughs. You'd get all dolled up in your finery and the fellas would dunk you in and all your composure would go. In a way, you went up there to see them.

The road became busier and because we'd be running across there was always the fear of a smack of a car or the fear that we'd drown. I don't really remember that part of the canal being filled in. But it seemed to happen very quickly. It was there one day and then when you looked it was gone, partly because people wanted it filled in, and partly because the hospital, St James's, was extending itself and their needs would have been taken into consideration. It was never meant to be a park for people.

We had a big protest over that because we knew that that road was going to become even busier with ambulances and cars. They put a hole in the wall for a gate into the hospital. We didn't get anywhere with our protest as the people at the back of Rialto thought it would be a good idea to have a short cut through to the hospital. So we were out voted and the wall went ahead.

Another thing that springs to mind and it's so relevant now. We used to go over to the hospital, and search through the bins and take the syringes out and have a great time sloshing up the dirty water into them and squirting each other. That's another thing we got a hiding for. You couldn't do that now obviously. Or else we'd go down to Guinness's and get the barley and take the end out of the biros and put the barley in and have great fun spitting at one another, taking the eyes out of one another.

Because there was a lack of playing facilities you made your own fun. There was skipping and beds or ball. You'd put the ropes around the lines and make

Lucy Johnston

swings and if the caretaker came along you'd be off up the pole, your rope would be taken and you'd be brought up to your mother for another hiding.

You couldn't ride your bike or you couldn't kick a ball or swing on the poles, especially not that. But as the pram sheds in the flats became disused, the fellas turned them into pigeon lofts.

There is a women's programme going at the moment and we're trying to organise things for the teenagers with Barnardos. From fourteen onwards there's nothing at all for them and we're trying desperately to address that by giving them a chance to say what it is they want, rather than assume and set something up that might fall through.

The fellas are into building lofts in a big way and that's the only interest they have. We're really afraid that when they start redesigning Fatima they're going to knock down the pram sheds, and then, where are the kids' lofts going to go? That's something we really have to look at.

The lack of maintenance has been deplorable, basically, they didn't care what you did. But now that it's all going to be dolled up and they're putting four million pounds into it, they won't particularly want pigeon lofts in it. Apparently you're not supposed to have that sort of thing in the flats.

In the beginning they were afraid of what you might pick up from the pigeons, or maybe they'd draw rats, so there was a bit of an outcry from the residents. And of course the droppings on your washing, but like everything else you get used to it after a while. People are concerned about the teenagers and rightly so, and they feel anything that occupies them and makes them happy is worthwhile.

The pigeons are alive and kicking. There are about four lofts. They were on the roof to start off but there were complaints. They didn't mind them in the sheds but they didn't want them directly over their heads. One man set up a loft in his front room. That certainly didn't go down too well either.

When I look at the kids now and think of what it was like when we were young I realise how innocent we were in comparison. It seems an awful shame that they have to grow up so much quicker. I mean, when we were still in our teens we'd be playing childish games. We had progressed from piggy and ball to kiss chasing and spin the bottle. You'd be waiting for the boys to catch you and hope the right one would, never running too fast away from them.

There just doesn't seem to be that innocence now. I suppose the kids just can't afford to be. Maybe it's my memory playing tricks on me but they don't seem to play games the same way we did. I'd see them an odd time having a game of skipping, where we seemed to be playing it every hour, on the hour, whenever we had a minute. Or ball, or piggy. Piggy doesn't seem to be played that much anymore.

I followed a family tradition and went to the Central Meat Products in Marrowbone Lane. It was a tinned meat factory and my mother had worked there and so had my three aunts and my granny and it was my first job. I was fresh out of school and I was pondering whether to go back to school or not, or should I get work. So I started going down there and of course when the money started going into my pocket, school was forgotten.

It was dreadful. There was no heating and you weren't allowed to talk to anyone. You had to hump out big pieces of machinery but the worst part of it was when they were making the mixture for the tinned beef. I'm going to turn people off tinned beef. I very rarely eat it these days. You had to lift it up and put it into the machine which put it into the cans. I remember coming across the little lumps in it and after two days of working there I had to fly into the toilet because my stomach was heaving. That was dreadful, although the hygiene was scrupulous and you had to be very clean.

I had a friend who had worked there before me and she had run out of it to work in a sewing factory. She knew how miserable it was but realised that I had the few bob and I didn't want to give it up, so she got me a job in the sewing factory. It was like going into paradise. I was delighted with it. You had heat. You could sit down and talk to other girls, and there was a radio. It was in Strand Street. Eirlaine was the name of it and it was run by a man from northern Ireland. I couldn't believe it that everybody would be complaining when I went in there first. I used to think, 'What ails them'. If they worked in the other place they'd realise. But again I became one of the great ones for complaining as well. We made skirts and blouses. Mainly skirts for Dunnes, and how they were ever sold I'll never know.

I worked there for three years and then I left and I haven't worked fulltime since. I started cleaning in the evenings just to supplement the income. At the moment we've applied for funding for me to work in Fatima.

So much has changed now. There doesn't seem to be the spirit that was there before. We're trying really hard to get it back again and keep people involved in their environment. I don't know how it happened. I can only think that people feel a lack of control.

We're starting afresh. We're trying to get people involved as part of a new project we're setting up to celebrate what we've achieved over the last six years. Most of my old friends live in the flats still, so we go out every now and again and reminisce and talk.

I slowly began to realise how far things had deteriorated. Older tenants could pin-point it to when some street was closed down and they started dumping people in. Anybody who couldn't be settled elsewhere was put into Fatima. The caretakers were taken out, they had always been resident. People slowly began to lose interest. Old tenants who had lived there from the very beginning moved out to houses because they didn't like what was happening. It became a bus stop for people either on their way to buying a house or getting a house. They really had no interest in what was happening and that, I think, is when the real rot set in. Now we are trying to reverse that.

A treat for us on a Sunday was to go down to Stephen's Green to the Dandelion Market. That was the only market of its type at the time and we'd all barrel down in a gang and just mess about or have a look around. When I compare that to the Green now and that monstrosity that they're building, it's very sad. All the character seems to be going and they seem to be replacing it with modern buildings. I don't even know how they get around to designing them. I mean just look at the Civic Buildings, the Central Bank, and now this one on the Green . . . I think they're deplorable, I really do.

They don't seem to understand that what they're knocking down is a very vital part of people's history and memories. They're just tearing away at it with no consideration. No remembrance or respect for it, something that was a large part of Dublin. I feel that that is what is happening all over. I don't know where these people are coming from or whether they're trying to make Dublin into a New York, which it's not. Dublin has a character all its own.

I got involved in community work when my son Owen was born. I started to take an interest in what was going on around me. I floated around for years doing nothing wondering what I was going to do. Then I became involved. It was like finding a little niche that I fitted into. There's a lot to be done in Fatima.

I began in the playschool. Then a feasibility study was carried out in Fatima because Dublin Corporation had been proposing a major landscaping job. Art Community and Education (ACE) sponsored a feasibility study to investigate play facilities for children. It's joint funding from the Irish Arts Council and the Norwegian Gulbenkian Foundation.

Annie Kilmartin was employed to work on that and I was part of the Fatima Development Association at the time. We went off to London to look at places, to look at adventure playgrounds for the kids. On our last day there we met a community architect and we showed him plans put forward by the corporation and we asked him where would be the best place to put a play space. 'Well, really ladies it doesn't matter where you put it,' he said 'because it isn't going to work. You're being offered a face lift.' 'Oh, you can't tell us that,' we said, 'We're after negotiating for five years with Dublin Corporation. This is great.' And he said, 'It's not. It doesn't deal with any of the fundamental social issues. It doesn't deal with why places like Fatima Mansions go into decay. People lose the pride they have in their area because they have no sense of ownership or privacy.' We told him he'd have to tell us more than this because he was giving us a nervous breakdown.

Then he brought us to a flat complex called Wakelin House. They had actually privatised the whole area and closed it off to outsiders and it was great, it was wonderful. We took slides and we came back to Fatima as nervous as anything saying, how are we going to explain this to people. But they saw it and people automatically know what is best and we decided to negotiate with Dublin Corporation for it. This is what we are doing. This is the direction that our negotiations have taken. We've made links with Ballymun and other flat complexes around the city so that we can show them what we discovered and how they can negotiate like us, because it really is the only way forward. We've done a lot of research into it. I stuck it out and I worked on it for two years, night and day.

In the end, we applied to ACE again for further funding to employ a local person to co-ordinate. Now within the plans for the design for the children, we'll be looking towards the youth and the elderly. These are all interfaced. You have the elderly afraid to come out because they're afraid of the young people at the end of the stairs and the fellas torment the elderly because they don't really understand them.

We want to get to the elderly because they have a story to tell. They have the history of Fatima. Part of the overall project would be a documentation of what's actually happening, but we also intend to get the history of people and what has happened in the past.

We also want to get the youth involved in a newsletter because sometimes you lose communication with people and the committee might be seen as a clique making decisions for them. We want to get the information out of them.

As a response to the drugs issue, which was a real problem in this area, we organised ourselves. We went to the people concerned and told them to either stop or get out. I don't know whether it's absolutely drug free but to the best of my knowledge it is. But there's always the possibility that there's someone there you don't know about.

We now have control of allocations and we allocate flats to who we like. That's brilliant and it has cut down on Fatima being a dumping ground. If we decide to house people that's our choice. We don't discriminate against people. Anybody and everybody is welcome. The only people we would be looking out for would be people who are bad addicts or don't want to be housed anywhere else. We definitely don't want drugs back in here.

The Millennium . . . I can't think of a word to describe it. I've been on the Youth in Community Committee and I have problems with it. The community should be the heart of what the Millennium is about. It shouldn't be a little committee set up by itself unless it's by working class people, because it certainly seems that most of the events are geared to the middle classes. I think it was a great little stunt. They'll get their motorway through the Liberties in Millennium Year. People will be out celebrating Dublin as 1000 years old, while, for other people it's a good deal older.

I think it's a tourist attraction, a PR stunt. I don't think it in any way reflects what's happening in Dublin or what Dublin people want.

I love Dublin, I love the people, I love the go of them, I love their honesty, the way they tell you straight what they're thinking of you. You know exactly where you stand and you've no illusions. I'm very very proud of where I come from. I'm very proud to be part of working class Dublin. I don't know about other areas of Dublin, I can only relate to the working class who face situations like we do in Fatima Mansions and compare with that. It's the people who make Dublin not just the buildings, but I feel with all this modernisation and buildings, that somehow something fundamental is going to be lost.

Stella Webb

I was born in Dublin on 30 August 1910, in Castlewood Park, Rathmines, then in the township of Rathmines and Rathgar. I can remember back to sitting in a pram, with a nurse at the end. I certainly remember the outbreak of the First World War.

In those days there was no radio, so if there was any special news the newsboy would come round from the side streets and the main streets and shout 'Stop Press.' I remember the gloom that descended on our house when the war broke out. Our next door neighbour, Mr Retz of Rathmines, a German pork butcher, was interned. Mrs Retz carried on the shop where we continued to buy our sausages. I remember hearing of the men coming to take him away but I don't know how soon it was after the war broke out.

The Quakers, and others, visited the German internees in the camp. I don't know if it was the Curragh then. I know it was the Curragh in the Second World War. I used to collect silver paper which was used to melt down and make things and I was given a little rabbit which someone stole on me.

We moved up to Palmerston Road. I can remember when going down to Rathmines, with the nurse attendant, watching the trams coming up out of town on a Sunday morning. My parents and grandparents would also come out. That was either the Terenure or Dartry tram. The Terenure tram ended in Terenure and instead of a number it had a red triangle sign up in front. The Dartry tram ended at Orwell Park. It had a red triangle with a white line down the centre. You can still see the tram sheds but they are now used by some company.

The Palmerston tram ended at Palmerston Park where the terminus still is today. I can't remember if it was a white circle or a white square. This route had very low bridges at Ranelagh so it didn't or couldn't have cover tops. It had open tops. The trams were all electric. When we moved up to Cowper Road they still had the low bridges in Ranelagh and I remember those of us who were hardy, on a wet day, used to go upstairs with all our rain gear on and the seats could go backwards and forwards. I always liked putting the seats facing backwards and sitting at the back. If we were going to the theatre, my mother liked to go inside on the tram and my father and I went upstairs and sat on the back of the seats, because the tram would be very full.

The Cross tram, which is now on the 18 bus route, had whatever circle or square the Palmerston didn't have. The only other sign I can remember is the Dun Laoghaire which had a shamrock. Then of course the trams got numbers before they changed to buses.

My father used to talk about the horse drawn trams and how, at Portobello Bridge, the tram had extra horses to help it up the bridge. Later we moved to the top of Palmerston Road, 3 Temple Villas.

I started school at the age of five. I had a convenient birthday in August. The school was run by Miss Tuckey in Frankfort Avenue. This was before the kindergarten ideas were in a lot of schools. She had taken over from a cousin of my grandfather, Gertrude Webb, who was one of the pioneers of the Froebel System in Dublin. Miss Tuckey's school came to an end in 1919 when she retired. The good will was taken over by Rathgar Junior School which is still run by Quakers in Grosvenor Road. Miss Tuckey was not a Quaker but a lot of young Quakers went to Miss Tuckey, Webbs and Douglases and various other people.

I was at the top class in Miss Tuckey's when she retired in 1919. Rathgar Junior School started with a top class a year younger than myself. I was sent off to Nightingale Hall run by Miss Wilson, in Wellington Place, at the corner of Clyde Road, and Wellington Road. She was very progressive with modern ideas of teaching. The only thing that we objected to was she didn't teach Irish. In fact she was what you would call a West Briton. In 1918 she used to have a great parade on British Empire Day. By the time I got there she had given that up. There was no flag waving. The building was taken over by St Andrew's. St Andrew's has moved on and I don't know what's in that building now.

There were more Quakers around then, about a thousand, than there are now. We lived mostly on the southside in Dun Laoghaire, then known as Kingstown. We had our meetings in Monkstown, we still have. Eustace Street, which has recently been sold to the Irish Film Institute, was a very large meeting. People didn't have cars so we went into town by tram as it was easier to go there. There was also a meeting for a time in Rathmines, behind Shaw's shop.

Meath Place, no longer a Sunday meeting for worship, was what we'd call a social centre. It was called the Meath Place Mission. They had Sunday School early in the morning. Gym classes were run by Edith Wigham. The Dublin Friends Badminton was played in Meath Place. When I left school it was full of Quakers, you could hardly get in if you weren't a Quaker. The Club has very few Quakers now. Mostly us young people in the twenties belonged to it.

There was another mission on the northside in Strand Street. The premises were then sold to the St John's Ambulance Brigade who have since sold it to someone else. My father used to teach in the Sunday School. He'd get up every Sunday morning at about 8 am and rush off. He said it was appalling. They had a lot of young Protestant children going there who knew nothing about religion except that they weren't Catholics. That was my father's report about the state of knowledge of these young Protestants. I imagine they had simple bible teaching.

My father was a solicitor and my mother was English. They married in 1907. Occasionally towards the end of her life she would say, 'You're awful. You awful Irish people.'

Lucy Johnston

Her father, an English Quaker, was very keen on Parnell and Redmond. My Webb family was very much in the nationalist tradition. My grandfather's cousin was Alfred Webb. He left the Quakers but had a lot of Quakerism in him to the end. He was a Nationalist Member for Waterford in the 1890s and was invited to India to preside over the Indian Congress at that time.

My great Aunt Josephine never married. She was an artist and to the end of her days she read at least ten minutes in Irish daily even when she was dying of cancer. So I had a great nationalist background.

I never got around to learning Irish properly myself. I could get by on the simple things of life. Unfortunately I lost a lot of it. I went abroad and tried to learn modern Greek. Then here at home I was dealing with elderly Russians trying to learn Russian, that overlaid the Irish which I tried to learn as an adult. The phrases which I learnt in my first school, Miss Tuckey's, I still remember.

I remember the great election in 1918. We had Sinn Féin, the Nationalists and Unionist candidates, and Rathmines was a stronghold of the pro British. But I recall a conversation over the back garden wall with our neighbours who were also of Nationalist inclination. The question was, 'Should you vote Nationalist for the person you didn't think had a chance, or should you vote Sinn Féin in the hope of keeping the Unionist out.' But the Unionist got in. He was the only Unionist who got elected in the south of Ireland in that election.

As for Women's Suffrage, I remember my mother and the woman next door were involved in a discussion about it but I don't remember her being involved with suffragettes. By the time I was really remembering the vote had been won. I knew certain people who had been suffragettes. I met Hannah Sheehy Skeffington. Owen Sheehy Skeffington was a fellow pupil of Miss Tuckey's. I met him again when I went to Trinity College.

I didn't get to Trinity until 1928. I was among the first women to do law. When I was doing my solicitor's letters over in the Law Society, there were five of us and about thirty boys. There was a certain amount of prejudice. I was apprenticed to my father and sent down with his law clerk who was a young woman. She told me that some of the old law clerks resented women going around the offices and would try and jump the queue in front of her. There was one particular clerk who didn't like getting into the same queue. Mostly she was accepted. I suppose my father was a bit unusual in employing a woman as a law clerk around the offices, but I didn't think it at all unusual. He just had two clerks. She specialised in going to the offices and typing and the other did accounts and typing. There was no trouble about it but it was a bit unusual.

I was asked by some northerners to talk about religious discrimination and I said, 'I have never met religious discrimination in my career but I did meet sex discrimination, often very subtle.'

I remember Helena Earley who was one of the first women solicitors. She was a great character. I knew her later on. She was tall and deep voiced and not afraid of appearing in court.

I was not involved in the Liberty Crèche but I knew those who were. There was a dining room there called the Meath Street Dining Room where they started serving penny dinners. The premises were owned by Lady Meath. About a year before I left school the young Friends discovered, one Christmas when the holidays came at the weekend, the Friend's Dining Room was going to be closed for three or four days. This meant that the regulars wouldn't get any dinner, let alone a

Christmas dinner. So they organised rotas to attend at the dining rooms when the ordinary staff were off for the Christmas holidays. This went on for years.

Anyone who remembers Dublin in those days will remember the news boys. They were called ragamuffins. Their trousers were obviously father's cut downs, and no shoes or stockings. I know there's poverty now, but you don't see that kind of poverty. Now you see boys selling papers with anoraks and boots or shoes.

I was sent to England, to York, for three years to a Quaker school called The Mound. My mother had been there. She had been brought up in the country by governesses and going there had opened her eyes to the world. So her daughter had to go there, too.

In those days, there wasn't much difference in exams between schools here or there. In a way I was sorry to have had that break from my Irish surroundings. I came back to Trinity, at the age of eighteen, a stranger.

Then came the troubles. When I left Miss Tuckey's I gave up the Irish because I was going to Miss Wilson. At first I was going to classes called the 'Likes of Me' run by Isabel Douglas who was head of Rathgar Junior School and very keen on the Irish. My mother was afraid, because of the troubles. Mothers are now afraid to let their children out after dark for other reasons but then, they were afraid of us getting caught in an ambush. I also remember that the talk round the Rathmines area at the time, was, that it was awful to be raided by the Black and Tans. They'd come into your house and wreck it. But if you were raided by Sinn Féin they would not do anything like that.

We did have a visit around 1920 from Sinn Féin. We had a very nice girl working with us. She was called a servant but she was more than a servant really. She was what would now be called a companion housekeeper. She was a very keen republican. A knock came to the door around curfew time. She opened the door and my father went to see who it was and heard her say, 'Ah ya needn't come here looking for arms, they're Quakers.' Well, my father went down and invited them in. All they did was to go to the drawers in the desk. My mother had a bad headache that day and was sitting by the fire. They apologised to her and went away. We weren't long in the house and we think her predecessor had a gun licence and they knew where the gun would be kept. But we weren't the right people. Anyway, I can certainly say if you were raided by the Sinn Féiners they wouldn't wreck your house.

I remember being taken in to O'Connell Street after the 1922 fighting. I was also taken in after 1916. We went down the next Sunday to a meeting in Eustace Street. A house had collapsed on the quays and you could still see a kettle on a grate up at the top of the house and nothing in front of it.

On Easter Monday 1916 we went for a picnic in fields out at Churchtown that are well built over now. We went back to get the tram at Dartry and there the men said, 'Ah there's no electricity, no trams. They're fighting in the city.' That's the first we knew. I remember being so tired and waiting to get into the tram. My father gave me a piggy back but my poor mother, who was also very tired, had to walk it. Later on my mother used to go in and out on a bicycle to the Quakers' place on Aungier Street. The supplies weren't getting through properly and they had a sort of a restaurant or a feeding centre and they fed everyone who came in. The feeding station was almost opposite Jacob's Factory. I don't quite know where it was exactly. I never pinpointed the place. It was easier for the women to

20

get in than the men. Sometimes soldiers, who were in Jacobs', came in.

My mother, Hilda Webb, my grandfather's cousin, Edith Webb, and Ettie Wigham, who lived at the end of Cowper Road, and other women, cooked meals and got food. A few men like James Douglas helped to get the food up from the country. I don't know how much is known about that place, but in 1922 it was well organised.

In 1921 we went on a holiday to Deganwy in north Wales, near Llandudno. We were on the same boat as Dev who was going over to England to have talks. There was a story then that the Protestant Archbishop of Dublin, Dr Gregg, was once arrested, or nearly arrested, because he was very like de Valera.

During the Emergency, I cycled across Ireland. Dublin was full of bicycles then, we all cycled everywhere. If you went out at night you cycled because the trams went off at nine or ten o'clock. That's when long skirts went by the board. You couldn't cycle home from a dance in them. I liked cycling because you got the smell of a country.

My father was very ill in the winter of the year in which the ESB was rationed. I remember coming home and finding my mother in the garden cooking a meal on a picnic fire. The rationing was so strict that I didn't have a bath for years. We kept any hot water that was going for my mother. In the end we got rid of the gas and got a solid fuel stove. There was plenty of meat if you could afford it, but it was very difficult for people who hadn't any money.

In 1945 I went to London and joined the Friends' Relief Service, which was a Quaker organisation and I was sent for a year or two to Greece. I was seconded to the United Nations Release and Rehabilitation Organisation. During the war the Friends' Relief Service was helping in England, running hostels for refugees. In 1948 I returned home to Dublin.

I don't like all the knocking down they are doing now but as someone once said to me, 'There were Jerry builders in the 18th century, same as there are now.' Some of the old Georgian buildings were well built and some were not. That's why the Quakers sold their Meeting House. We couldn't keep it up. It was a big, old rambling building and there was too much dry rot in it. The Irish Film Institute, which has it now, has to do a lot with it. We kept the houses, number four and five. The first floor is a meeting room for the small congregation that now go to Eustace Street. As I said, it shrank when people became more mobile with cars. Emigration is partly responsible for the decline in the Quaker population, but so also are mixed marriages. Of course they work both ways.

You ask me what do I think of Dublin. Well, I always loved Dublin. It is my home.

Cathleen O'Neill

Of the thirteen kids in my family I'm the first 'Liberty Belle'. We lived in one room over a shop in New Street up an archway. When my mother had six of us we moved out of New Street, yet we had only spent four years there. My mother had me, my sister Rose and then she had two sets of twins, one after the other, in three years. We moved when we were given a house in Ballyfermot. I remember the day my da said, 'Come on, we are going out to look at the new house'. We were in a bus which seemed to take half a day getting there.

The instant I saw the new house I hated it and to this day still do. There were steps up to the house. It was very impersonal. They only told me we were going out to 'look' at the new house, they didn't tell me this was where I was going to spend the rest of my youth. I thought we could have decided, 'We won't have that one'. I didn't see the need for a new house even though there was only one room and eight of us in it. I still felt I belonged to where I was. We could go down to the shop underneath which was, more or less, an extension of our living room. The people who owned the shop accepted us. I can remember all that.

What I cannot remember is my first ten years in Ballyfermot. It didn't matter to me. I think I purposely never made a friend. I never settled. I always came back to town, for my mam, to do the shopping. My da stayed at home with us because he'd been in the Second World War and had lost a limb, so he had an artificial one. We had an unusual childhood due to the fact that he was there and there wasn't that great shortage of money, which I'd have seen around me, neighbours, not even having the bus fare into town. But my mam spent a lot of time in the house minding the kids so in fact I was the one who did the going. I was the 'gofor'. I was the one who went into a pawn shop at age seven. I was the only child in the class who was excused school until 9.30 every Monday morning. Nobody twigged in the class where I was going. Sure I was going down to the pawn shop in Queen Street. It was Queen Street on a Monday and Winetavern Street on a Thursday. I would have been as comfortable in those places and as well able to bargain as anybody.

I used to go into town with my mam on a Tuesday and a Thursday for ten shillings worth of second hand bread. A pillowcase full of returned bread which they'd sell for half price; Halligan's on the quays beside Guinness's on a Tuesday and Johnston Mooney and O'Brien, in Bride Street, on a Thursday. Sometimes on a Saturday afternoon you'd get returned bread as well. But for ten shillings they'd fill a pillowcase full of bread that had been returned from the shops, supposedly a day old but sometimes it would be younger than a day old. Sometimes you got a cake or a bun, and that would be a bonus. That was two days a week for me and I was no more than seven or eight.

I was thinking back about town and how I felt about it. I felt that town, especially around Thomas Street, High Street and Dame Street, was my place. That is where I lived. Those were the places I went to for the bargains for my mam. I knew every second hand shop, every junk shop, every huckster shop. I knew them all by name. I knew everybody there. My library ticket was for Thomas Street. They didn't have a library in Ballyfermot so that was understandable. They did have one in Inchicore but I didn't go to that one. I spent more time in town than in Ballyfermot. I knew Marsh's library better than I knew the one in Thomas Street because I just loved it. When I'd go to those buildings I'd feel them wrapping themselves around me. It's not just a feeling of belonging, it's something deeper. It happens me around Marsh's library, all around St Patrick's Cathedral and St Audoen's. It happens me in other buildings. Some things I can't remember but the feeling of, 'this is my place,' goes further back than my memory.

While the Iveagh Market is not that old, in terms of hundreds of years, I still feel that it was my place and I'm very sad about the way it has changed. I remember going there with my mam to do the washing and hanging it up and drying it while we would go for the second hand clothes. I think the women in the Iveagh Market dressed every one of us. They knew us that well. My mam would pay for them but they would know her needs better maybe than she'd even know them. I loved the Iveagh Market. I loved the danger of it. When walking around the Market you'd see bedsteads piled high on top of each other and at the top of the pile you'd see a sofa.

I loved the mystery of it as well. You could escape in the Market. I can still see when I am looking in my mind's eye, six or seven prams piled high on top of each other. The dealers would know the contents of each pram and which one had their 'pokey'.

I cannot tell you anything about Ballyfermot except there was a playground up at the very top. It was opened by Dublin Corporation and I was sent there every single day of the summer holidays with the twins — the two sets, and Maria and Rose. That is where my mother sent us to be safe while she looked after the little ones. It seems a contradiction to send eight children under the charge of an eight or nine year old, but we were safe. They knew that I had to bring them. They did what I told them. We'd have our lunch, bread and jam and we'd always have our bottle of water. I can't remember the playground, I can only remember going to and from it. It was about two and a half miles of a walk. I don't remember anything about playground activities and yet there were activities because they used to open a hut and have painting on Saturday. I didn't participate because I was minding the kids.

I used to get every Sunday off and I'd come into town every single Sunday. I can remember that as plain as anything. I'd get one and six. Sixpence was my busfare. Again, you'd find me all around High Street. I didn't have to talk to anybody necessarily to feel I'd had a good day but I'd have had a good day, because the bookshops would be open. I was a people watcher even as a kid.

I started off school initially in Whitefriar Street, before I left New Street, which means I started school much younger than most kids. I still continued to go to Whitefriar Street. The bus used to stop at the Ranch in Ballyfermot and take us in. I began junior school in Ballyfermot. I remember the building was huge and I could never cope with its hugeness or the kids. I remember teachers saying, with a certain pride, 'This is the biggest school in Europe.' They also had the biggest classrooms. I remember sixty children in a classroom and I remember the poverty and the teachers asking you to stand up and say what you had for breakfast. If you said porridge or tea she would say, 'That was not enough.' But what were we supposed to do with that information. Take it home and say it is not enough? One day there was a woman outside the school selling apples for a ha'penny and there was murder over us buying the apples because they were cooking apples. But we were not as discerning as they were. We did not get the pains they imagined we were getting.

I went to Goldenbridge School when I was nine and did my Primary Examination there. I actually got a year at second level at Goldenbridge but then I had to leave. They gave me a scholarship, but the books and the uniform were always a problem. My mother got me bits of uniforms and I was beginning to feel self-conscious. It was the first time in my life that I had felt that way about my appearance. I was mixing with people who had uniforms and schoolbags to match and had paid for secondary education. I stuck that for a year, and eventually I left over typing paper, one and sixpence worth of typing paper. I was obviously bright and doing well at school. Every Saturday we did typing, bookkeeping and commerce and I didn't have any money for the paper. I was getting hassled by a nun and she just lost the head one day and told me I needn't come back until I had the one and sixpence for the typing paper. So I said, 'Right I won't be back,' and left. They sent for my parents during the week. They were very concerned because my dad wanted me to go on in school but my mam wasn't as keen. She wanted me to do what I wanted to do. She didn't see the value that my dad would have seen.

The nuns didn't apologise about the one and sixpence but they did urge me to come back. Nothing had changed; I still had the uniform that was too short and too tight, and I still had to borrow the books. Even if they had discussed a way of lending them to me maybe I could have gone back but as it was I didn't.

I worked in the Two Owls Tailors for two summers before my Primary Examination. I was twelve and a half when I went there and I got in because my da fixed my birth cert. The first thing they asked for in a place like that was your birth cert. I got the job there for thirty shillings and ninepence a week. Out of that thirty shillings and ninepence I got a half a crown for myself, which was a fortune. I stayed there for seven weeks each summer for the two years and I had a week for myself at the August Bank Holiday. All the tailoring shops closed down for August.

At fifteen when I had the row with the nuns the concession they made was to get me a job as a trainee telephonist in Crow Street, where the Golden Avatar restaurant is now, the Krishna's restaurant as my kids call it. I acquired the skill in two days. It was only a little switchboard and it was very quiet. I stayed there for two years but it wasn't enough to keep me going so I got myself a job in a shoe shop. After that I drifted back to the sewing because you could definitely earn money at that. My first real job was at a place in Hendrick's Street making children's anoraks. We used to say in the job that the anoraks were for spastics because if it didn't fit you cut it off. That was the joke in the place because you were on piece work and you didn't have enough time to go back to the cutter for alterations, so we remodelled the things ourselves. I worked there for two years and it was fabulous. Again it was in the centre of Dublin and I knew where I was and all around me. It was right next to Smithfield. Then I moved to another job in Aungier Street for better money and it was from that job that I married.

I was always one for going back to places of historical interest and, at fourteen, or even younger, I used to go to Kilmainham Jail and watch them working on it. Ordinary working men had begun to work on it themselves and some other people had set up a restoration society. So I went down there and by the time I was fourteen I knew everything about Kilmainham Jail. I used to take people around and act as a guide on Sundays. All my Sundays were spoken for. I loved it. I was there for seven years.

Looking at my own children now, at fourteen, I feel that they are not as mature as I was at that age. I was always very able and capable. I wouldn't let them out the front door! I was working with men and women three times my own age and was able to go up to them and say, 'I want to do this, I want to work at that,' and there was no problem.

There's a big difference between the Dublin now and the Dublin I was brought up in. I don't know whether it was ignorance on my part or innocence but I never felt unsafe in town when I was seven or eight. I remember losing my busfare in Francis Street once and asking someone for thruppence and it was okay to do that. I never felt unsafe. I felt I belonged. I felt I could cope with whatever happened. The people knew me. I don't mean they knew my name or where I lived but I knew their faces and, equally, they knew that I was from around.

My daughter Sinéad is sixteen and she had to work on me for a month before I would let her go into town to a teenage disco that started at seven and ended at ten. I really wanted to let her go but I was afraid. I actually said, 'I'll go in with you and come and collect you,' and she said, 'If you're letting me go, then you're letting me go.' Echoes of myself. Eventually I let her go.

The major difference for me between life in Dublin now and Dublin then is that I saw drunks in a playful innocent way. They lurched along the street and they never frightened me. Now it's not drunks you see but would-be muggers and rapists. I don't know whether my perception has changed or whether Dublin has changed. My kids today don't feel any of the fears that I feel. So in that sense I can't give you an objective view. I think Dublin has changed. I don't like the pool halls, the video games.

I live on the northside of Dublin now and I feel I belong there in a very real sense. Kilbarrack is my home. It has my stamp on it, and my influence and the influence of all my friends. We've done something in our own area for ourselves. I can see things that I've done all around me. I do belong. I've never felt any of that *angst* that most southsiders feel at crossing the river. Indeed I feel more of a northsider now than I do a southsider.

My interest in historical Dublin remained and my association with

Kilmainham did too, so that is still with me. My involvement in community development work began when I joined the Kilbarrack writing group. I couldn't do very much in the early years when I moved out there because I had big ones and little ones and I was very much engrossed in that job, the job you're supposed to do when you're married. But I wasn't myself when I wasn't involved. I read a lot and I was always scribbling away in the first ten years of my married life. The bulk of my reading was done in those years, in fact I learnt a lot during that time, most of what I know now. I was in a supermarket one day when I saw a book that was being sold by women who had published it themselves. Again shades of Kilmainham Jail, I wanted to do that. I said it to the women and they said okay. A couple of weeks later I wheeled my twin pram, with two nine month old babies, up the four steps into a primary school. They had a crèche which was a magic word. It was what persuaded me that it was possible to continue. I went in with all sorts of fears that I wouldn't be able to do it, that I couldn't write. But I felt I had a place to put my kids and that it was possible to learn anything if you had enthusiasm and the time.

I held the door of the crèche open, shoved the pram in, mentioned the kids' names; their nappies and bottles came out quite quickly and I closed the door, as much to keep them in as to keep me out. It was a real biggie for me. I can see myself there holding that door saying, 'You did it.' I was quite fearful about what I had done. I still had this working class thing about the kids being my all and there I was actually separating myself from them.

First of all I went into Basic English. It was something I knew I could cope with. But after a few classes the teacher said to me that I would enjoy the writing class a lot more. So I went into the class and from that moment I was committed to adult learning and development. From day one it changed me. In those classes I heard people saying things that I had been thinking for years, that motherhood wasn't enough, that house cleaning wasn't enough. I wasn't prepared to do that for forty years but how could I dare to say that, with a family, bringing up kids and married and with no real problems, except a huge sense of dissatisfaction with the job. I loved the kids. If I could only have been with them all day long. I actually taught the kids to read before they went to school. I felt that was my job and the other stuff, the nappies and the cleaning, was a chore. It didn't satisfy me, you could get it over in a couple of hours but I ended up stretching it over the entire day.

In the class I heard people put sentences around my thoughts. I heard the word feminism for the first time, even though in my own way I had been a committed feminist all my life and didn't know it. When I went into this group they were only kind of playing with feminism. But I was home. I had my place and I was home and I've never looked back. I've been involved with adult learning now for almost five years. Class is the issue we have now. Class is raising its head. For some, adult learning is seen as leisure activity, but for us in KLEAR, we see it as something for working class women, a way of developing. It can enlighten us about our situations, our families and help us to develop skills for a market. We enable women to take greater control of their lives and simply hearing someone say that this is not the way it should be, gives us freedom. To hear someone say that this life is lousy gives a voice to our thoughts and feelings. Particularly to women who have kids who are up in bed and who are not on AnCO courses. Now you don't even ask if the kids are unemployed, you ask if they're on AnCO courses. I think that that's a sign of the times. Isn't it?

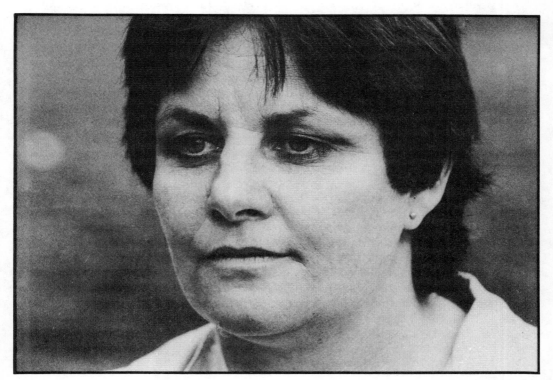

Lucy Johnston

Women in the home are our target. We want to get them out of the home and to allow them develop in some way. We're interested in early school leavers as well. They're the people who are losing out totally. They've no jobs, not even the possibility of an AnCO course. Something we used to laugh at years ago you can't even get now. They've nothing the poor kids. So we can enable them to question the society they're living in, at least that's something isn't it?

I would like to see communities responsible for themselves, actually managing their own affairs. In Kilbarrack there are five thousand homes and two blocks of flats. Sixty per cent of those in the flats are single mothers. They are alone and isolated and very vulnerable. You have young men, going in and out, who know the women are unprotected. I am concerned about this, as well as the fact that the schools are not properly integrated to cater for children who are disabled or slow learners. There should be a proper mix. People and children shouldn't be ghettoised.

There should also be third level education in the new communities around the city, relating to the cultural background of the people living there. I'm thinking of a Community Workers' Course which is something I would love to do myself. There's one in Maynooth but it's very expensive and would take two hours travelling time, which makes it impossible. That sort of course should be brought into the community because we could then use the learning for the benefit of the people. I would also like to see a proper bus service for the people of Tallaght and also, for the people there to get their long awaited and long promised 'Town Centre'.

As for the Millennium, it's just a nice big party. It means a free pint of milk, which I didn't even get, and half bus fare on the buses when I didn't have the other half. There's no acknowledgement of children that I can see; no talk of free activities or a crèche during the year; no supervised playgrounds. I'm very angry about the Millennium and the way children are being ignored. Why couldn't they have let the kids build the Lego City Hall? That would have been a great educational opportunity for the children. The Millennium, to me, is just like opening up your parlour while the rest of the house is in a mess.

Ellen Kennedy

I was born in 44 York Street where the College of Surgeons is now. We then moved up to No. 10 and 11 on the other side of the street. I was living there for a long time before they condemned the houses. We then moved back down the street to the reconditioned houses. I am living here now for 36 years. I had an aunt who lived with me, she died recently, aged ninety one. She was a marvellous woman.

The street has changed a lot since the time I was born. It is now full, with the College on one side and the new flats on the other where there were tenement houses. At the moment they are building a big shopping centre which will affect the area.

I went to school in Clarendon Street until I left at fourteen. I got a job in a sewing factory. Most of the women, or 'girls' in those days, nearly always went into something to do with sewing. All my friends and pals went into sewing. I worked there for about nine years, then they went bust. I went to work for Wrenshaws, which was down in Mercer Street, where they are building now. I worked there for about twenty two years. I liked it very much and I liked the girls I worked with. We had our ups and downs but who hasn't in factories? I didn't think it was hard work. We were in and out of work through slackness. I was also out of work because I hurt my back. Then we were made redundant from Wrenshaws and they moved out to Tallaght. They just stopped production and brought the materials in from England.

I was out of work for a long time but I did bits of cleaning jobs. I love cleaning. I was out of work in 1973, and in 1975 I began work for the National Social Services Board, then the Poverty Programme started and I went to work for them for five years. When they closed I was out of work again for another while. Now I'm back working again with the Poverty Programme.

Peggy, one of my friends from Wrenshaws, got married and now lives in England. By now most of the women from Wrenshaws are scattered all over the place but we still see each other from that factory even though we have left it a long time. Some of my friends, from the house I live in at the moment, went off to

England as well and most of them got married. A few of us didn't. Funny, when we worked in Wrenshaws some, about four or five of us, had to give up work to look after our mothers and we didn't seem to mind. At that time you did not get paid when you came out of work. You just had to somehow manage on whatever you had yourself, especially if your mother was a widow or an old age pensioner. You just survived.

When we left Wrenshaws some of us got better jobs. I remember the boss saying to me one day, 'Well Ellen, you're in a rut,' so I said, 'If I wasn't in a happy rut I would not be here. I like my job and if I didn't I would not be here.' None of us ever thought of leaving.

I went to the Holy Faith in Clarendon Street. There was a national school and a private school attached. None of us went to the private except one girl and I don't know how she did it. She was sent from the national into the private, she was the only one of the whole class. I think the school was good, we were taught by nuns. There were only two teachers, a Mrs Manning and a Miss Ahern.

Why they pulled that school down I don't know because it was beautiful. The nuns could not keep it going, they didn't have the pupils. Now there are a lot of young children coming into the area and they seem to be sent to Synge Street.

I got involved in the community around the neighbourhood and we set up a Community Residents' Association in 1982, which is still going. There is an awful lot that can be done around the area, like cleaning it up. There are eleven of us on the committee. We take in about ten blocks of flats and call ourselves the Whitefriar Community Resident's Association, rather than just York Street or Mercer Street.

The reason why there was no Community Association when I was growing up was because of the women themselves. My mother and her friends, gathered in each other's rooms. If my mother had a problem we were never allowed hear it because we were kiddies, you were sent out of the room, then *they* solved it. You didn't need a Community Residents' Association then. They had this neighbourliness which young girls have not got today. Nowadays the young women feel they are intruding. But it's the only way to keep in touch with people. The young girls won't come onto the association because they say they are not able to talk or they can't do this or that. The reason why we set ours up was because of the crime in the area. We got rid of a lot of it and then we concentrated on getting the corporation to do things.

We have a lot of new tenants in York Street, but there are still a lot of the old tenants there. Some of them are fifty years in Mercer House and they are getting very old. I don't know what is going to happen to the flats when they die.

Years ago you just lived in one room. You had a landlord whom you got to do things. He painted the house, the top part was red raddle and the bottom a black paint. Nowadays you have to pressurise the corporation to do it and do your best to keep your house in good condition. In the first house I lived in there was a woman who had sixteen children. I don't know how she managed but she did. Her husband was killed cleaning windows in Mercer's Hospital and she was left with all those children of school age to rear. If she needed help the neighbours helped. They hadn't anything but they were content.

I was talking to a neighbour today, a woman I grew up with, who said, 'I pity the teenagers today because they are very discontented.' We had to work for what we wanted. My father could not afford a bike for me, so I had to wait until I

Lucy Johnston

was sixteen to buy myself one. I appreciated it then because I worked for it. We had no labour, but then, there are no jobs now. Teenagers are not independent now because they depend on their parents. Around our way, when I was going to school, there was nothing but tenement houses in York Street. We occupied our time by playing in Stephen's Green. You can't play there now because of the courting couples. We played street games. We skipped for hours and played follow-the-tin-can. The streets always have a fascination for children and that's a fact of life. Children can't play on the streets now because they get bored and there is so much traffic.

I went to work when I was fourteen. We were all delighted. The pay was five bob a week for forty-eight hours and all we got back was a shilling. You could go to the Camden and the De Luxe for fourpence. If you were well off you went to the ninepenny part. You thought you were rich. I used to like going off on my own to the pictures or off for a spin on my bike up the mountains at night. When we got to seventeen all my friends went courting and some of them got married. I would not like to be a teenager today but I enjoyed my teens then. Children grow up too quickly now. There is too much emphasis on money. Everything costs money now. If you go to a disco it's all money. But the dances did not cost us much.

The College of Surgeons is good to the community. If we need anything, even their hall, they will lend it to us. If we need typing or copying it's at our disposal. I have that in a letter saying anything you need you can have. We look after them and they look after us. The church is also good to us. We started up a youth club and asked them if we could use the school to get the children off the street. The children were there two nights a week and they did not charge us a penny for lighting or anything. AnCO came in and did a survey to renovate the old school in Whitefriar Street. It's the boys' old school and will be 100 years old in two or three years time. The church gave us some money and is loaning us the building. The first priest we went to did not understand community work but the second did. There is a Clongowes Club in the area. We hope to finish in March or April.

There are two schools in Whitefriar Street. The new school was built onto the old school and it is the old school that we are renovating. It is huge and is taking a long time because we have come across dry rot and the devil knows what. We want to get the school involved because I find the more you give the more you get back. It would be good to get the children in the area to go to the school.

By being involved in the committee you get to know the people in the area. When I got involved first there were eleven men and four women and when they were picking out the Chairman and the Secretary I noticed it was all men. I said, 'Hold on there. There are four women here,' and that is how I got elected and I am still there. I find it interesting. We met the Lord Mayor and we met Garret FitzGerald who was very nice to us. We still keep in touch with Ruairi Quinn. We did not meet Mr Haughey.

When the Salvation Army came into the area Whitefriar Street was not a parish. Our parish was Westland Row. What happened was they got in touch with the Legion of Mary as they wanted the people to use the hostel. It was Captain Boyd who did that, he was very nice, he was all for integration. A very nice couple, they had one or two children. But he was shifted and the next captain did not want to know the people around. So it stopped then. There are two houses behind the hostel. We used to see the Boys Brigade and the Salvation

Army Band come down the street, but we rarely see them now. The hostel is not for down and outs any more. Now you work and stay there. Esther Boyce, a terrific friend, and her mother, Ma Boyce, would say to Captain Boyd, 'I don't mind you being in the Salvation Army,' when he'd ask her to pray for him.

I would like to see Dublin cleaned up. I think the people themselves should be able to say, 'I will clean up my part.' Some people think it should be left to the corporation. But if everybody did it we would have a lovely city.

The association was at a couple of meetings of the Millennium Committee but I found that they were inclined to stick with the upper class, if you understand me. At least the two meetings I was at, I felt that. Maybe in the summer when people have street parties it might work a bit better. At the moment all the functions are tied up with bigger people, rather than the likes of our community. At the meeting we attended they were all talking about the Vikings and that kind of stuff. You see you can't live in the past. You can remember the past. But you can't live in it.

Pauline Cummins

My parents bought the first house they'd ever owned in Cromwellsfort Road, Walkinstown in 1946. They moved there with their three kids. It was a rural area. I was born at home in 1949. I grew up there in the fifties and my initial memories of it as a teenager are of absolutely hating it. There was nothing to do, just walking around, no library, no community centre.

But then, when I thought about it again, I realised the incredible changes that have taken place and when I think of Cromwellsfort Road now, it's just a huge thoroughfare from one roundabout to another. It's just a traffic way.

There were three farms on Cromwellsfort Road when I was a kid and you'd go there to get milk and buttermilk. You could walk up the Green Hills and pick bunches of cowslips. Every weekend in the autumn we'd go off picking blackberries. So I've memories of being close to the countryside and to farming and having the freedom that you wouldn't have in the city to just race off into the fields.

When I was nine I was sent into school in the Coombe. That had an enormous influence on me, because of the freedom, the independence of actually getting on a bus on your own, paying your own busfare and trying desperately to remember which stop was your stop. That was my introduction to the city, and the variety of people that came to the school. Up to then I went to schools with people who were from the same background as I was.

There was the delight of being away from my sisters — I had three older sisters, but the exploration of meeting people who came from the northside, southside and centre city was exciting. They were from well off families. That would mean that their daddies were bookies or their grannies had apple shops in Kevin Street. But they were well off by our standards. They had sixpence everyday. I fell in love with the city from that period on.

The places I remember most are the routes that led directly from the Coombe to sweet shops. The big 'hit' was to walk from the Coombe up Francis Street to

Thomas Street and go down to Woolworths. They had huge displays of sweets. On the way were all the women selling different kinds of things. Just becoming familiar with all that commerce was a great education.

My sisters were ten, seven and five years older than me. They were really a totally different generation. It was that time in Dublin, in the world, where things got a bit easier. I was the youngest and I benefited most. Not only financially, my parents had more money, but the way you could dress as a girl, the dances, the way you could go out. I remember my sisters getting up on their bikes with these big beehive hairstyles and the net skirts and cycling into the city to a dance. After standing all night they then cycled home again, only to be stopped by the police for not having their lamp. Whereas, when I was a teenager of thirteen or fourteen I could walk to the local dance halls for the hops which were beginning then, in Terenure or Templeogue or even in Crumlin.

I was thirteen when I went to work in Lamb's in Bluebell. We walked from Cromwellsfort Road, through a valley. Up at seven o'clock to be there at eight o'clock. I find it extraordinary now, but then it was usual enough to see the kids going off to Lamb's. You'd work on picking the stalks out of the strawberries and if you found a black snail you got an extra penny. So it didn't take somebody long to cop on if you picked up every black snail you saw on your way to Lamb's and liberally distributed them through the strawberries you'd make a packet. You'd come home with red hands, I remember meeting boyfriends at the top of Cromwellsfort Road and hiding my hands. Being ashamed because my hands were covered in this red stuff and that wasn't beautiful.

It was really hard work and when you graduated from picking off the stalks you'd go on to canning. This was really much nicer but very dangerous. Hot tins with steaming hot juice would be flying around on this circular contraption and you'd have to get them off, once the lid was on, and get them into a container.

What struck me then at thirteen was that I had opportunities. There were girls there that I was working with and for them that was it. There was no other opportunity for them. Whereas I knew I'd stop and go back to school and have more choices in the end. It was a good thing to learn at thirteen.

I went to the College of Art and the woman who taught us was unusual because she'd let you do what you wanted to do in the art class. I used to like to sing when I painted and I often think that that's why I work the way I do, with sound and images. She'd take us out at the weekends, she was really extraordinary. I'd never seen a racing horse. She took us off one day, out Monkstown direction, to draw horses, and I remember that was the first time I met with bog land. Sliding down to sitting on your bum in wet land.

There was a girl in my class, Christine Broe, whose father had a shop straight across from the Coombe. She was really talented and, to me, a real painter. I had these ideas of what real painters were. The reason I thought she was a real painter and I wasn't, was that she painted buildings. She'd paint Christ Church or St Patrick's. I could no more paint something like that, because I didn't want to, but I thought that was what you were supposed to paint. What I liked was people. I was much more interested in what happened between people. If you went to the tuggers or the women who sold on the street and you bargained with them, well, I was interested in that but I didn't understand it then. But I do now. That was the real language that was going on.

If they said, 'Do you want anything love?' they were really saying, 'Don't mess

35

around here unless you're buying.' And if you were trying to get two apples for the price of one or they were asking for something it was the play of words that I was interested in. I didn't realise until afterwards that this was a form of art that you could show as well as buildings.

When I was going to dances people would say to me, 'Are you from the northside or the southside?' Now I never knew about the northside and southside. I think it was a city thing, the northside and the southside, or maybe it's something about me and direction but I didn't know anything about it. I knew about Bray and I'd say, 'Well where is Bray?' and they'd say, 'The southside.' I knew I was miles away from Bray and so I'd think I must be on the northside. Isn't it lovely logic?

I think we hit on something immediately when we started to talk to each other and that's snobbery. People in Walkinstown would look down on people from Crumlin and people from Crumlin would look down on people from Drimnagh. And we hadn't a penny to rub together, but everyone was trying to make their situation a tiny bit better than somebody else's.

When I went to the Coombe I didn't know snobbery. They had such a mix in the Holy Faith secondary where I went, that there was none of that. There was a healthy balance in my school and we were alright, but we didn't look to our right and see all the kids we never had any talk with in St Brigid's National School next door. We never mixed with them and the nuns were the bloody perpetrators of that carry on.

I lived in Walkinstown, then when I was about twenty-three I got a flat right along the quays at Queen's Bridge. Then I moved to Drumcondra, the end of Dorset Street behind Croke Park.

My father's grandfather was a baker in the Liberties. Isn't that grand? So we're three generations Dublin on that side. My mother's English. A good combination. I like it.

When I was pregnant with my third child I did a painting called *Celebration — The Beginning of Labour*. In it there are two naked women, running, carrying a pregnant woman high up in the air. It's meant to depict the excitement at the beginning of labour and the celebration that should take place in a community, in a society, when a woman goes into labour. The absolute joy of life. In the picture also there are women on horseback, calling, declaring the news and dancing and doing acrobatics.

On the one hand it's a simple depiction of the joy, but on the other it's a satire of the huge battle-scene paintings popular at the turn of the century where you have these thundering horses and men killing each other and mashing each other into the ground. It's both an opposite and a joke to say, here's the joy of life rather than the joy of battle. It's a big painting, it's eight and a half foot by five foot. I showed it in a gallery in Tulfarris, in Wicklow and I was very unhappy with this show. All my paintings at that time were about women, women being powerful, women being creative, and I was really pleased with them, and very proud of them. But when I saw them in the gallery I got a really sick feeling that they weren't going to be appreciated, that they weren't understood. The same demeaning of women was going to take place around my work because I was challenging that attitude.

The following year, in 1984, The Living Art Exhibition wanted to do site specific work. That meant that I'd choose a site and do a piece of work that was suitable for that place. I came up with the idea of doing a mural, a copy of the painting, in Holles Street Hospital. I realised I wanted the women who were about to have babies to see this painting. The feeling a lot of women get when they've had a baby is the absolute disregard of people for what they've done. Alright, you say, it's no big deal, you've had a baby, everybody has babies. But on the other hand nobody in the world would exist unless women have babies. It's not acknowledged enough, for my liking, anyway. So I decided to paint the mural in the courtyard of the hospital. That way the women in the hospital could see it, either while they were in labour or just after they'd given birth. It would also be seen by women going in for ante-natal classes and could also be seen, through an archway, by the general public without disturbing the hospital routine; it was also where the consultants parked their cars.

Luckily I persuaded the Master of Holles Street, even the word sticks in my throat, to let me paint the mural in the courtyard, and kindly enough he agreed. It took me four weeks to paint the mural. I had to prepare the wall. The mural was even bigger than the painting and I had to get scaffolding and an assistant. But what was wonderful for me, and why I never went back to the studio after that piece of work, was the physical enactment of all the feminist theory, the fact that I could get scaffolding, that I knew how to put it together, I could climb up on it and I was performing what in theory I believed in, in front of the whole hospital. In a way the hospital is like a feudal system. You've got the consultants and the matrons who are the real wheeler dealers. Then there's the doctors, the nurses and the kitchen staff and the people with the paint brushes and the ladders. These were my allies. They helped me out and took an interest in what I was doing. I took great pleasure in driving in and parking in the reserved spaces for the consultants. I felt I was a consultant in the hospital and I'd take out all my tins of paint and get to work.

All my kids were born at home. For me it was the most alienating thing to go to this strange building with your suitcase and kiss your beloveds goodbye and go in on your own. I used to think it was strange that they didn't have a welcome mat or a simple thing like having someone there to greet you and say, 'Isn't it great, you're having a baby.' I know it becomes routine for the people who work in the hospital. I appreciate that but I was really struck, in those four weeks, by the unhappiness, the unnecessarily unhappy atmosphere that could be in a place that really should be joyful.

Another part of the project, when I had completed the mural, was to put pink and blue ribbons through the railings, because so many people go past that building and don't even know what it is. I wanted to make a public statement of joy. I thought the pink and blue ribbons were a simple way of showing that girls and boys have been born there.

.That turned out to be great. I did it at seven o'clock in the morning so it would be ready for the rush hour traffic. You'd see all these motorists going 'ohooooo' because it was just all woven in and out through the railings. I started to tie these little blue and pink ribbons onto the railings and again one of the reasons why I didn't want to go back to the studio, was because I was constantly being asked questions. 'What are you doing?' 'Why are you doing it?' 'Are you SPUC?' Remember it was 1984 and that terrible referendum was very close to people's thoughts.

Some people thought the mural was a man who was dying for a baby and then suddenly his wife had a baby, a lot of romantic ideas. When they asked what I was doing, if I said it was anything about art, they would glaze over. If I said it was anything to do with celebrating having babies, it's to make sure that the city acknowledges what's going on here, then they could understand it. I didn't want to be the isolated artist away from the community. I wanted to look for ways to work in the community.

I finished the mural and I went away on holiday. Part of the agreement was that I would give the mural to the hospital and that was deliberate on my part. I wanted to see how they would behave. They painted it out. Immediately, within a week.

Now, if you walk past the archway to Holles Street Hospital, near the entrance to the car park you'll see a white wall where that mural was. There was absolute war and mayhem, in the hospital, between the sides that were for and against its removal.

While I was working there the fellas who wore the green garb would come down and say, 'It's great. You're doing great. They're going mad in there and the matron hates it.' Then someone else would come down and say, 'Such and such a one thinks it's pornographic.' They couldn't tolerate it. I don't know what happened, I got no explanation for it from the hospital. Mary Maher rang the hospital to find out why they had painted it out. They said that there had been a great many objections raised by the staff of the hospital who didn't think it was suitable, and some of the hospital governors also objected. Now, I'd say it was more the hospital governors. When did they ever take any notice of what the staff said?

The reaction I got from people walking in and out was varied. 'Do you call that work?' I'd say, 'Well you're going into labour.' They'd want to know if I had a baby. Had I the right to do that painting? When I said I had and that she was four months old the criteria for what art was and why it was being done changed. It challenged me and I had to come up with the goods. It was great for me but a shame that they painted it out. I often think I'd like to go back at night with a projector and project it onto the wall ... the ghost of a mural....

Traffic shouldn't be in the city. When I was a kid, in the 1950s, the centre city was part of a medieval city. Fishamble Street was still there. There was an atmosphere around the Coombe of Dickensian Dublin or its equivalent. People say to me the buildings were dilapidated looking, falling down and they were appalling and I wouldn't like anyone to have to live in them. But the atmosphere they created was, to exaggerate it, like a bouquet from a really beautiful bottle of wine.

The fact that the National College of Art and Design is now in the Liberties is magnificent. It's part of the community, not like when it was in Kildare Street, hidden away.

When I was eight or nine you could see the history, you didn't have to imagine it, it was there. Because of the doorways, the windows, you could see what it was like during the famine. You could imagine what it was like to have soup kitchens because you could see the signs to the poorhouses. The city walls were still there. I could see them, the Pale wasn't just a word in a history book. The Castle, where Red Hugh O'Donnell, who had a real appeal to me, was imprisoned, was there. To destroy all this is just unbelievably stupid, even from a commercial point of view. If people can't park their cars on the circular roads outside the city and be

bused to where they want to go then we don't deserve to have a city. People would come from all over the world to see a city preserved like that.

Elaine Crowley

When I think of Clanbrassil Street and how it was when I was a child it seems that it was always summer, the sun was always shining. I used to sit out on the step with my friend Hannah. There was a boy in the street we both hated and we used to plan to murder him, cut him up in bits, bury him. We were probably about four or four and a half at the time. We never told anyone about these plans, which was just as well because my mother would have killed us.

My parents, my brother, sister and I, lived over the Salt Shop. We called it the Salt Shop but I read in Thoms' Directory that it was the Salt Trading Company and the big blocks of salt were delivered there to be repackaged in the penny packs that were sold out in the shops.

My mother didn't like the fellows that ran it. She said they were two, cute, country fellas who were on at her in the beginning to make jugs of tea for them and they'd never give her so much as a penny packet of salt. It was a lovely street to live in. It was full of people who knew you and your mother and your granny.

I didn't like Thursdays. On Thursdays the cows came down the street. They came from outside the city somewhere and they were beaten on the backs by the drovers, then herded down the street, turned down Ducker's Lane to the slaughter house opposite the school there. Sometimes they'd break away from the drovers and run into the homes and try to get up the stairs.

My mother said that it was because they were terrified. They could smell the blood and knew they were going to be killed. They terrified me and although I've lived in the country for years, I'm still not all that happy crossing over a field where there are cows.

You were going up in the world if you lived in Upper Clanbrassil Street. There were considered to be great differences between those who lived in the street and those who lived in Gloucester Street and Gardiner Street. Nowadays people lump all those who lived in tenements together but within the poor there were as many classes as in any other group. And Clanbrassil Street was seen as a very poor street, but also as very respectable.

Shopkeepers who lived there were very comfortable. There was a little row of houses that must have been 150 years old, just next door to my grandmother. In there, were very comfortable tradesmen. It was very mixed.

Lots of beggars used to come round. Some would dance and sing in the street and the women would throw pennies and ha'pennies to them. But there were also regular ones who would call up to the house. There was one, a very upright woman whom my mother called the Lancer. She would never just come to beg. She always gave you a box of matches, a holy picture or something.

Then there was the one that my mother admired the most. She always described him as very respectable looking. He wore a dust coat, and a soft fawn hat and wore a hay coloured moustache. She used to put sixpence away for him out of her wages every week. He'd come on a Thursday. I'd often see him because I'd run out by her side. She'd give him the money and he'd raise his hat and say, 'May the loving and sacred heart of Jesus bless and protect you,' and she'd come back in and say, 'That's a decent poor oul fellow down on his luck.'

My father was very sceptical of him but she continued giving him money. That is, until years afterwards, when she was in town one day, she bumped into a friend of hers who lived on the northside. She used to work with her in Jacob's and she asked my mother over to the northside for a cup of tea. A knock came to the door and my mother answered it and who was there only the loving and sacred heart of Jesus man. 'Rosie,' she said, when she went inside, 'It's the loving and sacred heart of Jesus man.' Rosie went to see him and came back with an envelope and said, 'Ah no, that's Mr. Murphy. He has a very prosperous insurance business round on the northside. His daughter goes to school with my little girl in the convent on Eccles Street. They're doing elocution together and he came to give me a receipt for the fees.'

So here was this man with a prosperous insurance business, or told them so, on the northside, a beggar on the southside, and a lovely house up in Glasnevin and his daughter in a private school.

After I told that on the *Late Late Show* I met lots of people who lived on Clanbrassil Street and they all corroborated this story, saying yes, their mothers gave to him as well. So he made a nice little living for himself.

I lived in that street 'till I was seven or eight, then my father got consumption. Of course you never admitted it was consumption, he was just delicate or something like that. I used to go to a dispensary in the Long Lane to get buckets of cod liver oil which people believed was a great cure-all.

We left when it was confirmed that he had consumption because it was considered that we should have a house with separate bedrooms. We went to live in Kimmage, but my mother always felt as though she'd emigrated, even though it was only a mile or two up the road. She still went into Clanbrassil Street to do her messages.

I changed schools then, first to one in the village which had different classes of different ages in the one room, then to St Agnes' School, which in 1938 was supposed to be the most modern school in Europe. Then my father died and the first opportunity my mother had, she went back to Clanbrassil Street.

I went to Warrenmount Presentation Convent and according to legend it was once the Earl of Meath's house and it was to there that James came after the Battle of the Boyne. One of the nuns told us that when he came back he said, 'Your cowardly Irish soldiers ran away,' and the reply was, 'Ah, but your majesty has won the race.'

We walked in the beautiful grounds during the May procession. We'd all wear white dresses, our communion dresses, with veils. The majority of us wouldn't have white kid shoes, we'd have runners which our mothers had pipe clayed the night before. We'd have these lovely little wreaths to hold the veils on, little blossoms that looked like privet blossoms.

On certain days of the week we'd have lessons in the oratory. The oratory was lovely. It smelled of polish and a little bit of paraffin that they used in the heater.

On other occasions, I can't remember what they were, there was mass held there, and we went to it. The nuns' skirts would be pinned up on either side, with pins that had big black heads. They would take them out and their skirts would flow after them as they walked up the aisle. Like brides' trains. That was beautiful.

When I went to work I went to a Jewish firm of tailors in Cecilia Street. I didn't know, at the time I worked there, that it had been the School of Anatomy for UCD. In fact in one of Gogarty's books he writes of his mother or an aunt taking him there for an interview. Some of the other women who worked there have since told me, that when they started there, they found jars of pickled specimens. The only thing that I found, when I went down to the cellar to get buckets of turf, were rats.

We made suits and coats for all the high class shops in Dublin then: Horton's, Kennedy and MacSharry, and Seal's. There were about three clothing factories in the same building, terrible conditions really. We had a glass roof in the workshop where you roasted in the summer and froze in the winter, and a big pot bellied stove. We wouldn't bring anything like proper packed lunches, only bread and butter or margarine, not wrapped in greaseproof paper but in newspaper.

At about twenty to one we'd place all these packets on the pot bellied stove and the paper would start to scorch. By that time the bread would be toasted and the butter or marge would be melted.

We worked for so little money and worked so hard. We weren't allowed to talk but we were allowed to sing. The rhythm of the song helped you to keep the machines going.

On the other hand we were very well paid, comparatively. But we did work 'till one o'clock on a Saturday and we worked from nine in the morning till six at night.

During the summer, when they had a rush, you would be so thrilled to get two hours overtime you'd work till eight at night. I was fourteen at the time and so were many of us, but of course we considered ourselves lucky to have a job. It was rather like it is today. I regret it so much that the pendulum is swinging back and people now have to accept any conditions to get a job. It's something I hoped I wouldn't see again in my lifetime.

I suppose I wasn't getting any job satisfaction, but no one had ever heard of that word then. So I went away and joined the ATS in 1945 and I felt I had finished with Ireland. I was only in a fortnight when the war with Japan ended, and the war was over altogether.

The reason for going away was because I wasn't satisfied with the job and I had ambitions, which I didn't recognise as ambitions. I believed myself and my friend were going away because we were in love with two fellows. Both were much older than us and were great dancers and we'd hang around the edges of the dance floor hoping that they'd ask us up, but they never did.

Clanbrassil Street also had an exoticness about it. I didn't know it was exotic then but I knew that there was something that was different and exciting about it. This was because the Jewish community lived there, the shopkeepers. There were lovely smells, smells that were different, smells that were gorgeous, foreign smells. Sounds of different languages. They would get together and talk Yiddish.

My mother told me how, when they first came there and started up their businesses, some of them would 'get on their feet' as she said and would move then to Terenure and out to Kimmage and to the South Circular Road.

That end of the street was full of lovely smells. Smells of smoked salmon, and smells of the beautiful bread that the Jewish people would bake. There was one shop there, Ordman's, and they would have barrels of pickled cucumbers outside which a lot of the Christian women became very fond of. You'd be sent up to Ordman's to buy a penny pickled cucumber. They had smoked salmon. I never tasted that 'till I was grown up. But you'd see it and it looked lovely.

The Jews were very different in one particular thing; their men didn't drink as much as the other men on the street, so they were more comfortable. They mightn't have earned as much money but the men didn't spend it in the pubs, so they were very comfortable and very tidy people. At Easter it was great, the Christians loved the Jews to give them some of the matzos. Easter coincided with their Passover.

Then we moved to Lombard Street. There was a synagogue in Lombard Street and another in the Parade. We'd go and listen to the Jews. It was rather like benediction in a way. You'd hear singing and you'd see some of the very old rabbis, tiny men with very long beards. Men who'd come from Lithuania or Poland or Russia.

I think it must have been a very enriching experience for children living there. We had a fish market at the corner of Lombard Street. The dealers used to go up there on Wednesdays and Fridays, mostly to cater for the Jews who ate more fish than we did. We ate it on a Friday of course. Some would have proper wooden push along prams that they'd keep the stuff in. But the majority would use old prams. They'd buy their fish over in the Daisy Market and bring it over to the corner of Lombard Street, shouting their wares as they walked along. That's where I learned the names of all the different fish. The Jewish women would come to buy and bargain for their fish.

My mother had a saying about the Jewish community, 'They never forgot themselves if they got on well.' One in particular that I remember, Noyeks, became the biggest timber merchants in Ireland. They moved to Terenure or Rathgar I think. Because Clanbrassil was the street of their shops they would come back there to shop. On a Sunday morning all the shops were open, they would come and greet not just my mother but any of the women they'd been reared with.

I think I could say, and this is pretty general of all Jews, not simply in Ireland, they were never snobs. That doesn't mean that they don't want to get on and enjoy all the good things in life, but they haven't got this petty snobbishness of forgetting their rearing. The fact is that they worked hard to get on and they were prepared to work at anything, whereas some of us might feel too ashamed to do this or that. So long as they were working they were proud of that fact.

They were so kind to all the families there. One of the wives catered for weddings and things in the synagogues. She made food that we'd never tasted. Ordinary people in Ireland might make an apple cake or the Christmas pudding but that would be it. They used to bring this food home and give it to us. The most gorgeous pastries and breads that you'd ever tasted. They introduced a foreignness to the street, and it would have been the only street in Dublin where you experienced this.

The Jews were terribly maligned about money lending. It is true there were lots who did but the Jews were licensed and they charged a very fair rate of interest. The ones who were really the scourges of the working class women of Ireland were their own Christian neighbours who lent money. These were women who would get their capital out of insurance policies.

Years ago you could insure anyone you liked. They didn't have to be a relation. You could say to the insurance man, I'd like to take out an insurance policy on Mr or Mrs so and so and maybe you'd get a little money out of it, very little because the premiums were so small.

They lent the money and they worked on the principle that the woman's husband did not know about the borrowing. He didn't care what she did with the money except that he expected food on the table, three meals a day and she had to buy his clothes, in effect provide everything. The fact that she got into debt, he didn't want to know about. But if he did know, as they say, he would have kicked the head off her. This is what these money lenders traded on.

They would lend you two pounds and when you brought back the two pounds you had with it two half crowns. The money lender kept the two half crowns and gave you back the two pounds for another week. The next week you did the same and all the time there was the fear in your mother's heart that this would be the week when the hand would close on them, as they said. This would go on ad infinitum, paying the two pounds and the five shilling interest over and over as the capital was well paid. Unless you had a woman who thought, 'I can afford to tell my husband.' If you couldn't tell your husband you were in their clutches. They were the vultures and the vampires, not the Jews.

I came back to Ireland on my holidays and I suppose it wouldn't have been until the 60s that I discovered buildings were gone. The Pillar was gone, the Ballast Office was gone ... and I used to feel so irate. These things had disappeared without anyone consulting me or without my even knowing that they had gone. But like everything else you do get used to it. There was still enough of Dublin left to enchant me.

Then of course I wrote the book *Dreams of Other Days* and I came back to live here part of the time. I do notice what has gone wrong with Dublin. It upsets me very much. But as someone said to me recently when I talked to them about it, 'Ah but the bones are still there.' It's like when you meet an old friend that you haven't seen for a long time, someone that you love. As soon as you see them you notice all these terrible changes, but you only notice them momentarily. Then later you see all the good things that are still left.

This is how I feel about Dublin. I'm very sorry that some of the beautiful buildings are gone and that Dublin has followed on and made the same mistakes as some places in England. Bad town planning, knocking things down, not putting them up. Wherever you go there are stretches and stretches of dereliction, stretches of concrete where buildings used to be, or houses you knew, demolished, and their sites now used as car parks.

I discovered years and years ago that it's the people who make a city not the buildings. Although it's not common to be surrounded by people with Dublin accents, because there's been such an influx of people in from the country. Their accents are different, their children's accents are different too, since they are being taught to speak a different kind of English. Despite all this, there is this kindness and warmth. It's all over Ireland but Dublin is the place where I live and the people I have experience with. I don't experience it anywhere else. I've lived in Egypt, and Germany. I've spent years and years in England and some time in France. There's an immediacy about Dublin. Well, I could use the word magic, like two French people who were here last year. They could feel the magic. It's people and the light and the mountains, but most of all it's the people. It's the kindness and the concern and the warmth that comes through.

Once I went out to Balally to buy a pair of shoes and I'd rubbed my bunion. The girl who was trying on my shoes noticed and was so concerned she went into the chemist next door and bought some plasters. She actually put one on my foot. I can't imagine that happening anywhere else.

One of the most disturbing things I noticed when I came back to Dublin, was going into town at the weekend and walking down O'Connell Street and seeing thousands and thousands of young people. It appeared that you were always about to enter or return from a pop festival. I found that very disturbing to start off with but I've since got used to it, now I know that more than half the population is under twenty five.

We have so many wonderful values. We shouldn't try to imitate the English or the Americans or the Japanese with their efficiency or whatever happens to be the latest fad. There are marvellous values, values that are beyond price that we should cling on to.

The flat I lived in over the Salt Shop is knocked down. The grate that my mother used to black lead is lying now amidst the rubble and the stones on the bottom floor, with the grass and the weeds growing in and twining around it. When she didn't have enough money to buy black lead to keep it shiny she would keep a fat piece of bacon and rub it over the bars.

The house across the road where my grandmother lived and where my mother was born and married from, that is now a very upmarket antique shop. There's nothing left in the street. It's so hard to remember that it was once a thriving community.

When we moved back from Kimmage I used to live in a place called Rosedale Terrace. My mother called them the houses with the long gardens. Before the Jewish shops were built they had long gardens that went right out into Clanbrassil Street. There were five or six houses in there and there was still a green in front. Then the corporation, during the mad time when they went around condemning everywhere in the 60s, condemned these houses. They were about two hundred years old and they could probably have been saved, renovated. There was a woman who lived in one of these houses who kept ducks. The walls were three feet thick. Now it's full, packed with rusted cars and scrap metal.

Clanbrassil Street in the 40s, although it was right in the city, had a countrified air. At the back of one of the dairies there was a haggard where they used to graze cows. We used to play in there as children and there were two cows in there.

Then the bees would come and we'd catch them and pick wild flowers. There were dairies in the street where you could go in and get a glass of milk and new laid eggs, hot from under the hen, as my mother would say. Now it's gone, knocked down. I think they're going to build a motorway down it.

It had lovely names too. There was one place up the top near Leonard's Corner called Chestnut because at one time chestnut trees grew there. They had a little turn off called the Parade. I think those houses are protected. Wonderful names, Lombard Street, Vincent's Street. Further down there was Bonney Lane and Fumbally Lane.

I'm delighted to be alive in this year of the Millennium, and I think it's wonderful we are celebrating it. The particular part of the city, where Dublin had its origins, I've always known very well, loved very well, even as a child. I was always drawn to it, perhaps because I was reared very near it, and I worked very near it. I'd spend my lunch hours wandering through the little streets and alleyways, down Winetavern Street, down to the quays, walking along them all. I like to believe that I have this second sense. I don't know what you would call it, but I can sense in a place the life that has gone on there for a thousand years or more.

Twink

I was born and grew up on the South Circular Road and I went to Scoil Bhride in Harcourt Street, an all Irish speaking school. It has been knocked down since and they've relocated the premises. Then I went to Beaufort, in Rathfarnham, because we moved to Templeogue. Some people still remember it was a village that you got a bus trip out to on a Sunday. When we moved out people thought we had lost our marbles. 'How could you be moving out from a grand central place like the South Circular Road to the country?' Templeogue *was* the country, there were five houses on our road. It really was the wilderness. There was a bus every two hours! There was no bus from Templeogue to Rathfarnham — there still isn't. That's progress for you.

It was terribly difficult to get to school in Rathfarnham. I had a pony at the time and we were seriously thinking that if there was a place in the grounds where I could tie it up, I could ride it to school. For convenience, and a lot of other reasons, my father moved me to St Louis in Rathmines, which was a fortuitous move because that's where they discovered I could sing. Heretofore, I had been known as a dancer. It helped if you could sing because the nuns were very music conscious in St Louis and I walked into the plum job of lead singer with the choir as I had the advantage of also being able to play the guitar.

My memories of school in Dublin are wonderful. I won two scholarships, one to St Louis, in Balla, Co. Mayo and the other to St Anne's in Milltown, Dublin. I decided to stay in Dublin so I chose St Anne's. During this time I was travelling with 'Maxi, Dick and Twink', all over Europe. We were very popular as kids. That started to cause problems in that it meant taking time off school, a week here and a weekend there. I had this absolute lady of a reverend mother, who, because she put it so nicely, mortified me. She used to say, 'Now, you know my dear, I'm not one to stand in the way of talent, but you are not Sister Herman's pupil now,' which was a dig at St Louis.

My mother and father were in Pell Street Musical Society. I believe Pell Street was the name of a street in Show Boat and they called it after that. It was a grand old musical society. My cousin Monica is the secretary of the Dublin Grand Opera Society and my father's sisters are into the classics, Our Lady's Choral Society, so there was always music in my home.

During my early childhood we lived in London and it was there that I started ballet classes. When I came back to Dublin ballet was a bit thin on the ground but we did manage to find a ballet school in Stephen's Green, Baby Medlar's. I'm sure a lot of Dublin people will remember going to Baby Medlar. I had a marvellous teacher there called Jill Margie. I did ballet and tap with a friend of mine who is now a dancer in London, John Sullivan. Then I went to a Miss Ryan for Irish Dancing. I went to the Jennings on Camden Street where I did ballroom, old time and Latin American dancing. I even represented Ireland a few times as a kid in different places.

Theatre kids in my day were gleaned from the ballet and dance schools. We would be auditioned, as is usual, and if you could sing and dance you were really flavour of the month. Looking cute, singing and acting was all part of it. They always used professional stage children for the pantos, children like the Billy Barry's. They still do. I'm raging I didn't go to them as a kid, because they are responsible for turning out some marvellous artists and wonderfully disciplined children. They are the most charming, delightful, well-mannered children you could possibly meet.

I never remember the thrill of going to the Olympia that people talk of now. I suppose that was because I was always in the shows, as opposed to being at them, on those Friday nights. It seems to me that there was far more of a tradition of going to the theatre among the ordinary people then.

I also don't think there are as many children now in theatre as when I was in training. When I was growing up in Dublin in the late 50s dancing lessons cost money and people just didn't have that kind of money. There was a great community spirit and there was the garage concert. A lot of kids learned from each other. They never went to a class but they could tap and Irish dance terrifically. These children would go to see their friends on stage and, whereas, they were as good, dance wise, they wouldn't have the discipline needed to be performing on the stage.

There were the Oultan Kiddies and we were the Gaiety Kiddies. The Olympia had their own. I did the odd thing for the Olympia, they had a clatter of cute kiddies, Connie Ryan's Cute Kiddies. That's who Maureen Potter was weaned with. They were really the only stage school for children. The incentive wasn't there, apart from the mad rush of Shirley Temple, when every mother wanted a darling child who was cute with ringlets and could sing and dance. When that fizzled out, the reality of the cost of dance lessons hit the pockets and that was the end of that.

When I was a child, the people who ran the theatre, like Eamonn Andrews, Fred O'Donovan and Ursula Doyle, were very strict on the children. They made it quite clear to our parents that they didn't want to get any letters of complaint from schools. They would not hear of the theatre being used as an excuse for poor homework or poor reports. If that was the case, then sorry, the children were out. It was very good for us. We used to bring our homework in. We had number ten dressing room up at the top of the house. When we were infants we had the back room off the Royalettes dressing room. Can you imagine? What a way to grow up.

The Royalettes were great. They were part of growing up, the real Dublin ones, with their great wit and humour. They were fantastic, every word a gem. When we got to the ripe old age of nine or ten, we were considered too old to be in with them, we weren't babies any more. We were then shifted up to number ten

Lucy Johnston

51

dressing room. There were big costume skips that would come over from Bermann and Nathan's, London. We all had our own little skips and we used to sit in them between the matinee and the night show. We'd buy our burger in Robert Roberts, across the road from the Gaiety, now defunct, and minerals up in the Green Cinema and then we'd get into the skip and do our homework.

It is regrettable that you can't bring people back from the dead to tell stories about Dublin. There were two old stagedoor keepers, Mac, in the Gaiety, and Albert, in the Olympia. Both have passed on, sadly, but they regaled us, as kids, with stories about Dublin in the 'rare old times'. In the winter, when I'd be doing the pantos, my father would come and collect me from the theatre. In the summer we would go home in taxis. Daddy would be sitting at the stage door and every night, going home, he'd tell me another yarn that Mac had told him and I'd say, 'Ah, sure, I know that one. Mac told that to me himself.'

Both old men hand picked their stories and up to the time Albert died he would come up to my dressing room and carry my bags down, like the old gentleman he was. The last show I worked on with him was *Oliver*, in 1980, in the Olympia. He wouldn't hear of me carrying my own bags, protest as I may. It was an insult to him not to let him do it. Every night, from the dressing room to the stage door, he'd have some yarn to tell me, right up to the day he died. He had so many memories of Dublin and Dublin characters. I might not have known Bang Bang or any of those people but Mac and Albert were two great Dublin characters who made a lasting impression on my childhood with their story telling and tales of Dublin.

Many a good artist started out by winning local talent contests. If you read a lot of biographies of artists you will see that they won the Marymount Hall Talent Scout Contest. I remember Patricia Cahill talking about singing in the Marymount Hall and other marvellous artists talking about the local parochial halls, when they were kids. The amateur musical societies are still struggling on bravely and I think it's a good thing for people who can sing, they need somewhere to perform.

Every city has its own smells and I would say that Bewley's is one of the pleasanter Dublin smells. But what to most people might have been an unpleasant smell, was to me the smell of home. It was the mixture of the smells of the Gaiety Lane. The smell of the theatre on the left hand side, the smell of Sawer's fish shop on the other side and the smell of urine in the middle. As unpleasant as it may seem to people, that unique blend of smells was a part of my growing up in Dublin.

When I think of those lovely old houses on York Street and the condition they have been let go to. My grandmother talks about the grand ladies going to the ball and the carriages pulling up in York Street and the ladies coming out in their gowns. A beautiful old street and they were lovely old posh town houses.

My nana was a grand old Dublin snob and we used to go with her down to Bewley's regularly. I loved watching the man roasting and grinding the coffee beans in the window and the smell of the coffee would be everywhere in Grafton Street. I remember, too, going up to Findlater's to watch the man make the butter up with the wooden pats. All those lovely memories . . .

I was sad to see the rapid deterioration which had set into Grafton Street. It was as though a massive termite had gone down the street and destroyed everything that was wood and real, to make way for plastic. But I am now thrilled to see some sense of the old world creeping back into the street. It's taking a turn for the better. We have probably Brown Thomas's bravery to thank for that, in returning to brass and wood. The lovely old paving, and the lamps, are bringing back some air of respectability.

O'Connell Street is a thundering disgrace. What are these people in city councils and planning agencies doing? They are ruining my beautiful city.

My parents speak with great fondness and love of the Theatre Royal, where they both performed. My father gets all soppy and misty eyed when he talks of it. He'll wax poetic for an hour about the Royal and how tragic its loss is for Dublin. Sure, they wanted to knock down the Gaiety, up to a few years ago, not to mention the Olympia. Only that marvellous idea of the brick for a pound saved it.

We are such a cultured race and turn out so many artistically talented people. Major playwrights, musicians and poets. We have some of the best literary minds in the world and we export them all over the globe. And they want to knock the theatres down. It's like slitting your wrists. They want to cut off the blood supply. The Gaiety and the Olympia are two magnificent theatres. Visiting artists who come over here will say to you, 'What a beautiful old theatre.' They are lovely to work in and they are a credit to the people of Dublin.

There is something about Dublin. I met a friend called Louis Walsh — he's Johnny Logan's manager — before Christmas in Grafton Street. The street was ablaze with people, lights and colour. RTE had a big mobile disco outside the HMV store and the kids were buzzing around. We went into Giordani's for a cup of coffee and when we walked out Louis said to me, 'Do you know what it is, but I love this old city. There is nowhere in the world like.' And I said, 'No, there isn't, there is nowhere like it.'

Dublin is a unique city. It has a charm and a magic and a charisma all its own. It is absolutely unsurpassable.

Deirdre Kelly

My home was in Leeson Street and one of my earliest memories, strangely enough for a city child, is of herds of cows coming up the street. Somewhere near us there was an abattoir. I can remember, when I'd see the herd of cows coming, I was so afraid of them, I would lock myself in the bathroom at the back of the house. I could picture them coming up the stairs after me and even as I got older, I never lost my fear of them. I always felt that they were old bulls.

Another memory, which highlights the difference between Dublin then and now, is being with my brother, who was three and a half years younger than me. One of our games was to sit with our noses pressed against the window, counting the traffic. We would have a competition. He would take the traffic in one direction and I would take the other. Very often we would have to wait about ten minutes for a car. We would get very bored with this and say, 'Okay let's count vans,' and when no vans came, we'd count buses. It was during the war years and it shows the small amount of traffic in Leeson Street then.

My father was an unusual man. He was a great reader and he also painted. He worked as a bus driver but he also kept a little bicycle shop down in Hatch Lane. This was a centre for everybody, including university students and policemen from Harcourt Street Station. I think he did more talk than work. We were never sure if he was a bicycle shop owner subsidised by being a bus driver or a bus driver being subsidised by a bicycle shop. All I know is that we never made much out of either of them.

At the corner of the street, right beside where we lived, big open air election meetings used be held, very near what was Walker's pub and Caldwell's shop. My father was in Clann na Poblachta for a while and I can remember him wiring up microphones through our bedroom window, for the platform down below.

The side window on our landing overlooked what used to be Mespil House, where Mespil Flats are now. If you looked across, you could see Iris Kellett's Riding School. I used spend hours at the window looking at the horses, another animal I'm afraid of. It was really beautiful, on a summer's day, to look over the big, big trees of Mespil House, which had a river running through it, and watch the horses jumping.

One of my first memories of the destruction of Dublin, was watching, from our window, Mespil House being demolished. Our father was outraged at the idea of it being knocked down. Nobody made any public outcry about things like that in those days. I watched the walls coming down and my father said, 'Watch, this will be the last wall.' Next thing, there was a big cloud of dust and there was no more Mespil House. It was the first time I ever saw a ball and chain being used.

It is hard to believe now, that Burlington Road would have been a place where kids played. It was so quiet. You would never see a car. There was a lamp-post and a tree, where the road branched off to Mespil Road and Waterloo Road. All the kids would go down there on their bikes and skid. Chestnut trees lined the road and at that time, Leeson Street was practically on the outskirts of the city. You did have Donnybrook but you weren't too far from the countryside. You just had to get on a number 11 bus to Clonskeagh and you were in the country. Clonskeagh waterfall was a place we went to play quite a lot and I once had a funeral ceremony there for a bird which I buried underneath it.

The canal was very central to my growing up. The stretch between Leeson Street and Baggot Street is where we usually played. We were always warned never to go there but it's where we usually played. There were steps, which seem to have disappeared now, going down into the canal. My father told me that they had been put there specially for the swans, so I always referred to them as the Swan Steps, even as I grew up. I am sure they are still there, under the mud. There was also a big hollow tree, called the Bogeyman's Tree, which I used to get into with my father and we would 'boo' out at the people passing by. I'm sure they thought he was crazy.

One memorable day, I was crossing the canal on top of a table with a crowd of youngsters and my father happened to be driving his bus over Leeson Street bridge. He stopped the bus on the bridge, jumped down out of his driver's pad and ran down and yanked me off. I must confess, when I was halfway over, I was hoping someone would do it because I couldn't swim.

The canals were much sprucer in those days because they were used as commercial waterways and were cleaned, from time to time, with dredgers. In the 1940s, enormous horses, which seemed like elephants, walked along the banks, pulling the boats. When they came to the bridge, the horses were unhitched and they made this terrific clonk, clonk as they crossed over to the other side, where they were hitched up again. The men had to push the boat under the bridge, with a barge pole, and then through the lock.

Each section of the canal had its own set of swans and very often there were swan fights. I saw one particularly vicious fight at Leeson Street bridge. The swans had their necks wrapped around each other and were fighting like mad. The weaker one was left lying on the bank. I rang the zoo, who agreed to have it, and I asked a local taxi man to take it up there.

Sandymount was complete happiness to me when I was a kid. I went there every day during the summer, unless it was pouring rain. My mother and the woman upstairs and all her kids, and our kids, would walk all the way there. It didn't seem anything in those days to walk to Sandymount, down Clyde Road into Ballsbridge and down Sandymount Avenue. Now, if I suggested to my kids that they walk to Sandymount, they would have a fit at the idea. Walking home, of course, was another matter. We had to be dragged.

Hundreds of people would come to Sandymount every Sunday and we used to sit over at the baths watching them. They'd have big pots of boiling water and egg sandwiches. At that time, Sandymount was part of every Dublin child's life. I remember when they built the wall to take the pipes. I felt so outraged when they were allowed to take away the lovely strand. Sandymount was never the same.

When I was growing up, Dublin was an intact city. The big difference between then and now, is the pace of life and the destruction of the city. Admittedly, in the 1940s there was terrible poverty. A lot of places that have been knocked down, needed to be, but others didn't. They just needed to be renovated. The bad thing about that is the loss of the communities in the city. No matter where you'd go in Dublin one community might be better off than another, but they were still communities with their own type of history.

Take Upper Leeson Street. As well as ourselves, we had the students living there, with University College only up the road. That's another thing that has changed the city — the loss of the students and UCD. I think it was a great mistake to move them out to Belfield because it changed the whole atmosphere in the area.

Baggot Street used to be marvellous. It had both a city community and a cosmopolitan community, with families who had been there for generations and writers and artists from Dublin and elsewhere. People in Fitzwilliam Street were well off, but in Baggot Street they were a mixed bag. I moved there twenty seven years ago and it was teeming with life. Now it's all offices. If you cycle through it from town at night it's like a tunnel of darkness, with no lights in the windows. That's what a city becomes when people give way to the demands of commerce.

I've always regretted the passing of the little local shops and huckster shops which were all over the place. They were great institutions. Apart from selling everything from a needle to an anchor, they were social centres for the local women, places where they gathered around the counters, chatting, exchanging information on this and that, helpful and otherwise. You really got to know your neighbours in those shops. This is lacking now in the suburbs and large housing estates. People are isolated. They can't get to know each other like they used to.

City Quay, Westland Row, Merrion Square, all that area, which was once a wonderful place to live in, has changed completely. The few communities left are just struggling to survive. They know that some developer is going to come along with enough money and political pull to get the houses changed into offices. Leeson Street is full of discos and the mainly elderly population living there are going through hell. Permission for these discos was given by various Ministers for Local Government who also over-ruled the corporation and gave permission for the building of huge office blocks.

There is no attempt being made to control traffic. The attitude is that people who own cars must be allowed to use them, so motorways are more important than the preservation of community life. The fact that 82% of the people living in the inner city don't own cars, is totally disregarded.

In 1969, the Dublin Housing Action Committee focused attention on the appalling housing situation in the city and at the same time the Georgian Society highlighted the destruction of the classical buildings of Dublin. What had been forgotten was that there was more to living in a city than being housed, although basically, that is the most important thing. But the communities were being

Lucy Johnston

destroyed too. I thought that a group should be formed to focus attention on this, so, together with my husband, Aidan, and Margaret Gaj, we decided to do something about it.

I contacted people like Geraldine Murphy, who was active in the City Quay and Westland Row area, and the Living City Group was formed. The basic aims were the preserving of the communities and the planning of the outskirts of the city. Bad planning and urban sprawl have been allowed to destroy the beautiful hinterland. However poor we were, when we were young, we could always get to the country very quickly on a bike or by bus if you had the penny fare. Now, that has all gone.

Another of our aims was to bring back the City Architect, which we never succeeded in doing. There is nobody to take responsibility for the mess that Dublin is in, the buck keeps passing. One of the reasons why we don't have an architect is that when they did advertise, they didn't offer a big enough salary to attract a person with the necessary experience. Now they seem to have stopped looking altogether. They keep saying that they have a City Planner and that the City Manager runs the city, but he is not an architect. His attitude to things like offices and roads, as well as the issue of crime and its effect on the city, is questionable.

I don't think the Millennium will focus attention on the real problems, it's just window dressing. It's a good thing in a way to brighten up the city, but when you have alongside of that, the council giving planning permission for roads that are going to destroy Clanbrassil Street and Patrick Street on the south side and North King Street on the north side, how can you celebrate? The window dressing is for places like O'Connell Street where no one lives. But then, authority in this country has always been on the side of commerce and the living core of the city is being sacrificed for commercial interests.

Hopefully it will generate some money from tourism and the like, but I doubt that the money will go to the right places. When you look at our city hospitals closing down, kids living homeless and when people like Willie Bermingham are finding old people dying in basements, you can't really work up much enthusiasm for dolling up the city, can you?

When we started off Action Inner City in 1970, there were very few groups around, but now, nearly every residents' association is conscious that they are living in a community and they are very aware of their rights. They have a tremendous amount of power, voting power and lobbying power. I think that the hope for the city lies in these groups, particularly if they use their power properly. Unfortunately, what the people can do is being undermined by lack of money. Most groups and organisations are operating on a shoe string. A simple planning appeal costs £36.00 and that is a lot of money for a small association.

I think the whole road situation is the final death blow to the city. We'll probably find a few stalwart communities that will survive, but on the whole Dublin will be broken up. We may, in some day or time in the future, architecturally, bring the city back, but we will never bring back the feeling of Dublin as we have known it — that special thing, which was Dublin.

Nuala O'Faolain

Do you remember a *Late Late Show* about Dublin, a great *Late Late*, that ended up with an old lady dancing with Gay Byrne. As I was watching I was thinking that by those standards I'm not a Dubliner at all because that was all about the real old Dublin people who call themselves old Dubliners. People from the Liberties or people from the inner city who can look back generations in Dublin. I felt really excluded from that even though I was born in Dublin. When I'm asked if I'm a Dubliner I never say I am. I say I was born in Dublin but I grew up around the place.

My father and my mother came from the same street in Drumcondra, Clonliffe Road. It is a long street that comes down beside Croke Park, a very typical Dublin street. It was all red brick and very respectable, even though when they were young it was all outside toilets. They met sharing a taxi and their parents were really only about two skips off the bog. My father's family was from Wicklow and Mayo, but they lost links with that and my mother's family was from Kerry and they lost links with that. So they must be very typical of people who moved to Dublin around the end of the nineteenth century and led that first expansion of Dublin. They weren't really Dubliners and they weren't really country people. Really they just led family lives very, very quietly.

My granny didn't even know her way around Dublin. She just knew a few of the shops. She'd go into Hafner's every week to queue up for sausages. She went to mass every day and knew the other old ladies who went to mass. Her friends were in service and she might get a tram, once in a blue moon, out to Rathmines, to see her friends for a cup of tea. She would never go in the front door, but around the back. She would not have known where anywhere in Dublin was. She knew nothing about governments and their politics. I doubt if she really noticed when Ireland became independent. I remember asking my granny, when I got old enough to realise that she was valuable because she was old, did she remember 1916. '1916,' she said, her face all wrinkled up with distaste, 'Oh yes,' she said, 'there was terrible trouble in the city you know, awful stuff going on, shooting and all.' Then her face brightened up and she said, 'It was a wonderful year for vegetables.' She explained that the carrots used to come into Dublin from north County Dublin and Rush and they couldn't get in because of the trouble in the city, so they all stocked up in Drumcondra and all the ladies went up Clonliffe Road. 'I'll never forget,' she said, 'the vegetables in 1916.'

What they did remember was Bloody Sunday because, of course, Croke Park was just up the road. My aunt, who would not, even to this day, know who rules Ireland, remembers standing up in the parlour and watching the silent crowds, absolutely silent, with tears coming down their faces, walking down Clonliffe Road away from the massacre at Croke Park. Neither family had any link with public life or any interest in public life. They just lived their own lives and never made any noise, quiet as mice.

My father and mother were not like that at all. They were gay old things, bohemians. When they got married they had no money, so they used to move from house to house up on the borders of Dublin and Meath and up to places that were entirely rural then, between Malahide and Portmarnock. We grew up in various residences in the country.

To us, we went *in* to Dublin. We went in to Dublin to see the granny. We commuted for hours every day, sometimes to go to school in Dublin. When there were rail or bus strikes we would be left in Dublin which I thought was the absolute height of magic and glamour and wonder. I used to stand opposite Ballybough Flats when I'd come in from the country and long to live in a flat, because the country was so miserable and dreary and lonely and we'd walk miles and miles to school in bare feet and it seemed to me that Dublin was wonderful. Kids playing on ropes and everything. No one does that in the country because there are no lampstands and there are no other kids.

I thought Summerhill was wonderful with its big high tenements. It was so sociable, everyone sitting on doorsteps and living so close instead of being stuck out in the miserable fields. When I was nine and ten I used to go on huge walks around Dublin by myself, to Smithfield and up around Guinness's brewery, just looking because I thought city life was so interesting and beautiful. I loved the texture of Dublin, I still do, it used to be all smoky gleams of sunlight. I loved buildings. I did not know the difference between a good building and a bad building but I just loved the streets of Dublin and I longed to live in Dublin. But when I was young we never did. I was just moved around and we ended up in a miserable small town and I got into loads of trouble with the police and I was sent off to boarding school up on the border.

While I was away at school my family actually moved back to Dublin. When I was sprung from school at the age of seventeen it was the beginning of my own life in Dublin and that was at the end of the 50s. What I was supposed to be was a student at University College Dublin (UCD), which was then in Earlsfort Terrace, right in the middle of Dublin. My real links with Dublin are from the four years it took me to get through UCD, with dropping out and being expelled and having to go off to England to earn the money. Those four years at the end of the 50s and the beginning of the 60s are what I would call my Dublin. Being a student then was quite unlike being a student now.

My three Dublin lives were, first, coming in from the country just to admire it as an outsider; my second was when I was a student. Then I went away again. I mostly worked in England until about ten years ago, when I came back. The last ten years are my third go at Dublin. I really love Dublin, but it's a completely different place each time.

Nowadays when people think student they think separate, a race of young people who stick around together, have haunts of their own and dress their own way. But we were just in Ireland's Dark Ages. It was still the 50s and the young had not been invented. For example the word teenager wasn't known of. Furthermore there was no such thing as money. We had no money at all. We were students in the sense that we went into UCD and were supposed to go to lectures, but there were no tutorials. Nobody knew if we were there or not. Above all we had to earn our living and you *could* earn your living then. You could be a waitress or work in shops. I was a shop assistant everywhere.

Those were wonderful years, very mixed up years, but they were years of very cheap bedsitters in places that are now all offices, like Nassau Street or Stephen's Green. I remember hearing Mendelssohn's Violin Concerto for the first time in an American girl's bedsitter in Stephen's Green. We were all supposed to live at home and most people did, but only sort of, because like my own home there were so many there anyway. There were another eight besides me and there really wasn't room apart from when somebody went to England, which everyone did. You were not exactly thrown out and you didn't exactly leave, but you drifted around. In the first years maybe you'd walk home at night — five or six miles, to Clontarf in my case, but gradually you'd stay over and gradually the rows about not coming home would get less frequent and then eventually you moved into a life of your own.

Trinity students, when they lived outside college, were supposed to be inspected by some class of a proctor to show that they were single sex households and very respectable. They were very far from being respectable. There were huge amounts of sex in Dublin in those days. Vast amounts all over Dublin in those very dark, very damp warrens where we all lived and moved around. It was as if the whole country was breaking free, mainly through sex which wasn't talked about, not even between the bloke and girl, but it went on day and night. There was no contraception or nobody knew about contraception. It was just your tough luck if you got pregnant. If you got pregnant you had to marry the bloke. You just *had* to. If he wouldn't or couldn't marry you then you had to go to Belfast to have the baby and have it adopted, which happened to quite a few people.

I do realise that the great majority of students in UCD lived perfectly respectable lives and went to dress dances and so on, but the world I was in was not respectable at all. It was terribly interesting. Music is terribly important to the young now but we didn't have any music. We'd never heard of Irish traditional music. There was no music. There was a lot of drinking. There was a lot of lovemaking. There was a lot of talking and the talking was good talk, full of ideas, full of people teaching each other things, lending each other books. It was a very curious world. It must have been like nineteenth century Paris because we all sat around in damp old coats. We didn't have any interest in clothes. We were often hungry. I know there was a whole year when I didn't have a coat until a man I met at a political meeting bought me a coat in Switzer's. My first ever new coat. The same man bought me the first steak I ever tasted and my first coffee with bubbles in it, because coffee was quite a new thing.

There was no great distinction between young and old. We used the same pubs as older people, much more distinguished people, but they didn't think of us as awful young people. If we could afford to buy them a drink that was grand. If we were in their company that was okay. You got used, later, to being in the Red Bank or even very occasionally in the bar in Jammet's where you could get a great big plate of pea soup quite cheaply, or in McDaids or any of those bars where there were poets and writers. Nobody made us feel that we didn't belong there too. We were all equal, middle aged and young, equally strapped for money and we all returned bottles, even for pence. We were trying to pick up bits of jobs, in their case they were writing reviews, on the backs of paper bags, which they'd collected a few quid for. In our case we were looking for work in restaurants. We all drank as much as we possibly could and the city was a very exciting place full of passion and talk and love affairs and drama. I know from outside it must have seemed that there was a huge difference between Trinity and UCD students, but down in this underworld there was no difference.

There was no difference between UCD and Trinity students. The only difference was that Trinity students had rooms. This was an unapproved-of life. No parents knew about it. There was something about the poverty of Dublin then and the poverty of all of our families, except for a few unionists from the north, that does away with extreme moral attentiveness. Nobody was free to keep an eye on us. They were only barely struggling to survive themselves.

There was a kind of moral watchdog at work in UCD and I got expelled for unbecoming behaviour at a party. The moral censor then, is now a television personality. He personally expelled me from, I may say, my only chance at higher education. While on the one hand people like him were throwing you out, on the other hand the women who worked in the offices in UCD were letting you back in again. A priest gave me the price of the fees and eventually I got another scholarship.

It's not my own history that matters here, it is the way things were. It was all very inefficient and personal. The 50s were almost tangibly breaking up and by 1961 when I was doing my BA and I had fallen in love and was formally living with a married man, still there were moral censors, still people went to my teachers to say would they stop me and one very good man tried to do his best for me. He actually paid in advance for a bedsitter for me in a respectable house to stop me living with this bloke. In retrospect, of course, he was quite right because if I had become pregnant my life would have been completely ruined. But I did not know that, I was completely in love and by 1961 everything was quite different from what it was like in the late 50s. It was not that I had grown up a tiny little bit because I had hardly grown up at all, but the years had been so fragmented and dramatic that you did not know whether you were coming or going the whole time. Still, it was just about possible, particularly with bohemian parents like my own, to stick it out and insist you had a right to love and to make your own decisions.

In the house we lived in on Baggot Street there was a young woman who was secretly married to the son of a very famous Dublin family. He would sneak over to see her for a few hours every night. Because his family was respectable, and hers was not, the marriage was unknown. There were all kinds of liaisons warrened away in houses. There was a woman who had a baby but she went around with a pillow under her skirt because she had to pretend she hadn't had the baby. The whole dreadful, dreadful 50s thing that there was no sex and that nobody got pregnant before marriage led to so many secret lives. Dublin

connived with these secret lives. There were huge houses in Pembroke Street and all along the canal; all the Georgian streets where there were twenty or thirty people, twenty or thirty different secret lives in each of those houses. All of them hiding from official Ireland, all of them ready for the 60s. There were also very respectable business ladies who lived in bedsitters and always had done, and had little coal fires. They were the heads of cosmetic counters or they were something in the civil service and gradually I came across them. They took a little drink privately.

I remember those years in Dublin. It was terrible what I was doing to myself but, sure, I didn't know that. They were worth it because of the number of people who would introduce you to the poems of Housman or who'd tell you about the Famine. We'd never done the Famine in school. We knew nothing about Irish history. We used to work like mad for Noel Browne. We used to sit in the cold offices. I remember an election he contested in, maybe, 1959 for the National Progressive Democratic Party (NPD). Lots of us canvassed for him. David Thornley, Proinsias MacAonghusa, all kinds of famous people and people like us who never before had a political notion. Politics meant nothing to us except that Noel Browne was right and that poverty must be abolished. I remember canvassing off, what I now realise, was Meath Street. We thought we were living in poverty but I didn't know there was such poverty. I mean there was Russian poverty in Dublin then, like Moscow before the Revolution. It was unbelievable and so was the ignorance of the populace. We were ignorant, but bleeding God, they kept calling Noel Browne a communist. People like Frank Cluskey kept breaking up our meetings. There were still faction fights.

On and off then, I was away from Dublin in the early 60s till the late 70s. And when I came back it was as a grown person, with a job in Dublin and enough money to buy a house. After all it was the first time I had money in Dublin. Then I realised that I didn't know my way around this city. I still don't. If I'm anything I'm a northsider because of the few years my family lived out in Clontarf and I do know the backstreets of the seafront there. To this day I wouldn't know how to get to Templeogue. I'm not sure which one's Crumlin and which one's Cabra, and I bet you someone from Crumlin or Cabra doesn't know much about Clontarf or Dollymount. For all that it's a small city, you never seem to command more than a tiny little bit of it. When you do (if you ever do) get a car, then, you have to learn a little bit more.

But Dublin still surprises me. It's so changed from my granny's day. It's so changed from when I was a student. So many of the streets have been stripped of life by office blocks, by horrible office blocks, that you have to search the city for little pockets of ordinary Dublin vitality. It's almost like being a tourist now, to go down Thomas Street or Meath Street. And in my memory all the streets used to be like that. The Victorianness of Dublin is gone, places like the Dolphin Hotel and the bars we used to go to. They were heavy wooden Victorian bars, and now, more and more bars are of an international style.

Another thing that's different is that the young people are a separate population now, and the dance halls are all gone. My friends and myself, from Clontarf, used to go to the Sunday afternoon dance at the Metropole and then go to another one in the evening. We'd dance, dance, dance. Dancing of course was the merest cover for courting afterwards up the alleys, against doors, against lamp-posts. Extremely erotic, those days were. I don't know what happened to a whole nation that was obligated not to go the whole way, but went as near it as they possibly could.

At least dance halls were human, you could see the blokes coming across the floor. They weren't really very drunken places. I gather they were in rural Ireland, but in Dublin they weren't really. I know there are discos now but there aren't those great big bleak dance halls where you could nearly hold up a banner saying you were a woman waiting to be felt up. And the men could nearly have held up the same banner.

I still love Dublin. I love it very much indeed. I feel it now as having this terrible hinterland of big cruel estates. I feel Tallaght, I feel Clondalkin and I feel Kilbarrack stretching out around Dublin and masking all the happiness and exuberance of the centre city, which does still exist, with a kind of mocking. I preferred Dublin before the estates, but there's nothing can be done about that. If people have children it will happen.

The Millennium? Why not? These are just cooked up PR things, but on the whole their intention is good and good humoured. I can't see what possible harm it does, and I'm all for its little events.

Muriel McCarthy

My earliest memories are of Clontarf, where I was born. I am very lucky because I have a twin sister — we are identical twins — and I regard that, of course, as a great bonus. So, I suppose, we are Dub. twins or twin Dubs., I don't know which. I do know that I am very proud of being a Dubliner.

Clontarf, at that time, was not at all built up. There were quite a lot of of fields around and I can certainly remember playing in Mr Maloney's field. He had cows in it and he used to supply milk. That was an interesting thing about Dublin in the '30s — the number of people who were engaged in supplying milk in horse drawn carts, with steel milk churns. Desperately unhygienic! They had something which they called a 'tilly' and when they gave you a pint of milk, they also gave you a bit extra. Like the Christmas box you used to get from the grocers years ago.

My mother sent me to school very early, but my memory of that school was that it was really primitive. My father was from Donegal and he spoke beautiful Irish. The state had been formed and he was very nationalist, so he was determined that my sister and I should go to the new Irish schools. My brother went to the Christian Brothers. My mother didn't have the same strong views at all. She realised, that as twins, we were very small and perhaps a little bit fragile. She thought the school very overcrowded and she pestered my father until, eventually, we were sent to the Holy Faith Convent. We were very happy there.

My father died and we moved into the centre of the city, into Merrion Square. You couldn't imagine anything more magnificent, a big Georgian house, very comfortable to live in. There were many people living in the square then, many families. We used to have great fun playing in the park. It was beautiful, with marvellous facilities and hiding places for games, like relievio, that could go on for hours and hours. It was never crowded. The park belonged to the Archbishop of Dublin and the residents paid a small rent and got a key.

In the summer, walking along the square, you could see the other side of the coin. It used upset me to see a lot of people outside the railings with their families. Now, that was really disgraceful, no doubt whatsoever about it. Holles Street was nearby and the people lived in appalling circumstances. I remember scenes of great deprivation on my way to school. Passing Brereton's pawn shop on Monday mornings, there was always a queue of women with their husband's suits and other items, putting them in until the weekend. I know people are badly off now but I really don't see anything as awful as I saw then.

Towards the end of the war, I can remember going to school and the terrible cold and trying to light the wet turf. There was no central heating in the part of the school we were in, only this damp turf fire. We had to have coupons to buy clothes and we had to try and scrounge an extra bit of tea from the grocer or maybe some sweet biscuits. Earlier on I remember being given a gas mask. I suspect that a lot of Dubliners of my age have such good teeth because there were very few sweets or biscuits then. I can still remember the luxury of getting a banana or an orange. And white bread! That was extraordinary, seeing your first white loaf.

But as usual, people overcame all these regulations and restrictions. I remember going down the country, like all Dubliners whose parents were from the country, to the house of a friend of my mother's. She took this silk stocking and sifted brown flour through it until all the white flour came out then she made fairy cakes. I'll never forget the delight of seeing those white fairy cakes!

A little adventure on the way to school was to walk over the lock gates of the canal, holding on grimly as we walked across. Of course, we were told not to, but it helped to make our trip to school a little bit more exciting.

The other memory, for my generation, is the final years of the war, hearing about what was happening. There were the air raid shelters that were built in Upper Mount Street and in Merrion Square, absolutely horrible things. In Merrion Square there were four shelters, two underground and two on the ground. One of our delights was to lift the cover off the underground ones. They weren't tied down, because, I suppose in an emergency they had to be opened fairly urgently. We could look down and see the water flowing down below and we knew that if there was an air raid and we were ordered in that there was at least two feet of water in the shelter. We could see the toilets made out of bins floating in the water. We used drop stones down into them. I wonder what they did with them, did they ever fill them in? They may, in fact, still be there.

We were very small when the air raid happened on the South Circular Road. My mother was a widow, there were four of us, and I remember how very frightened she was and how she tried not to let us see it. She came into the bedroom and we were all there and she prayed. She was very brave. That particular night was terrifying.

When I got married I went to live on Palmerston Road which I loved because it is so beautiful. But then Charles and I bought a house in Raheny, which was a little village then. Later it became very built up. Even though I was in Raheny for twenty five years, I really felt in some way, that it wasn't quite my place, although it too was beautiful. So, when I got the offer to come in and live in Marsh's Library, we discussed it and accepted. I do feel enormously happy here. There's something about being in the centre of the city, of being with the Dubs and coming back to the village atmosphere. The shops across the road, Camden Street and Meath Street, now, that part of the centre which I know extremely well, must be the most exciting part of the city. Of that I have no doubt whatsoever.

There are no supermarkets in that area. As far as I can see the shops are still owned by individuals. You go into the butcher's and Mr. Hogan knows exactly what you want. Then you go into Cullen's and they know the sort of fruit and vegetables you want and, of course, Carmel's, the off licence and all the other little places, like the drapery shop. Right along the way, they all know you and greet you. It is an extraordinary thing to find that village atmosphere still. I think that in some parts of Paris you might get that. Dublin is warm and welcoming and it's very, very exciting and there is no doubt about it, there is a Dublin wit. The mispronunciations and the crack and friendliness. I was talking about that the other day, the way the Dubliners are calling the Millennium, the Aluminium.

The dereliction of Patrick's Street, though, is appalling. I can't see the reason for it, or for the way Clanbrassil Street has been allowed to go down to, really, the pits. It's heartbreaking for me to walk up around by Patrick's Park and to walk up by Werburgh Street, just beside where Swift lived, and see the queues of people outside the Labour Exchange. Young people, middle aged people. I have no doubt that they are dying to work. There are some who are unable to work for all kinds of reasons but in general, the majority of people in this city, indeed, in Ireland, want to earn a living, want their dignity.

I would very much like to see more employment. It's heartbreaking to see the diminishment, because that's the only word for it. Unemployed people are diminished in Dublin. There's a different kind of poverty in the city now, from the one there was when I was growing up. My father was a civil servant and he had, what I suppose was an average income, but the war years, those were a great leveller in Dublin and in Ireland. Everyone had a ration book, unless you could overcome it in some way and, of course, there were always people who did that. But, I think there was much more equality at the time. That is not so now. You can see people here these days who are very rich indeed and then you can see the people who don't have much money.

I am convinced that a lot of people, if they were given the incentives or were allowed to, would come back and live in the centre of the city. Look at all the houses, look at all the shops that are on the ground floor, and then, just lift your head and look on top as you walk along all the main streets in the centre of the city. Why is it that tax incentives cannot be given to people to decorate their premises? There are lots of skilled people who could reconstruct and do up houses themselves at quarter the cost charged by institutions like the corporation. I'd like to see Dublin improve and become more pedestrianised and I think it could be changed without too much spending of money. I mean, there are awful advertising signs that could be taken down. By removing those alone, you would be able to see certain buildings.

Living in the inner city does have its problems, like the bag snatching and the stealing of motor cars. I'm not sure why this happens but I seem to remember that it didn't happen when we were growing up. But now, you see these big supermarkets in the city and these huge displays of the most exotic kinds of food. Now if you are unemployed and you have children, it must be very hard to see these displays and to have to pass them by. People in my time didn't steal, they didn't break into cars. I'm not excusing it but it must be very hard when you have a family and you walk into these supermarkets and you see others filling up their

trolleys with everything they want.

The drop in the Protestant population is very sad, although the school across from St Patrick's Cathedral, has a long tradition and is a very fine school, seems to me to have a great number of pupils in it. In fact, they come from all over Dublin to it. I think that the contribution of the Protestants to Ireland, to our culture, and the different way they think about things, has added to the enrichment of our society. You have to come together, you have to recognise, you have to discuss, even if you have to give way slightly, there's nothing wrong with that. And we must recognise that their contribution to our culture was a very rich one and we are lesser people without them.

I think the Millennium is a very good idea. When we are down economically to some extent, why don't we have a party? Why don't we cheer ourselves up and celebrate what we do have, anyway? There are some wonderful parks and buildings in Dublin. Just to walk along O'Connell Street, even though it is so grotty, and pass by Trinity College, Nassau Street and Dame Street, at least, if you ignore some of the things at the top of Dame Street, well, you might be quite happy.

There is still the beautiful Bank of Ireland, the marvellous job they did on it, the Ulster Bank and the Arcade in George's Street and Powerscourt House. It's very exciting. Let's get on with the positive approach to things. Look at the Royal Hospital in Kilmainham and indeed, my own institution, which was refurbished, thanks to the American Ireland Fund. Let's be aware of the good things we still have in Dublin.

People are definitely more aware of what you shouldn't do. I know it's very upsetting about Wood Quay. That caused a great deal of distress. When you think of all those people who went on all those marches, like the Provost of Trinity College, F.S. Lyons, academics, solicitors, writers, bankers, right across the whole spectrum of our society. People came from everywhere to show their disapproval. It's upsetting that it didn't work. But in this way it has worked. There's no doubt about it, if you go to do something nowadays, you do it at your peril, because it may cost you a great deal of money and trouble. People who are in the money-making business are not going to get caught out, they are going to think about it a lot more. So in that way it has made people more aware. I am proud of the Millennium and I think it's a great idea. I'm all for it.

Mary Mooney

The quality of life in Dublin now is different to what it was when I was a child. I was reared in Oliver Bond which at the time was one of the biggest flat complexes in Dublin. It was right there on Ussher's Quay. It always seemed to be summer when we were kids. We'd be out first thing in the morning 'till last thing at night, and you were safe. Even if it was eleven o'clock at night and you went outside, went up to the forty steps you'd be safe and nothing would happen to you.

I remember Corpus Christi when we were small. The flats were painted, they whitewashed the stairs and all the pillars around. Anyone who could afford it would paint their door. If someone had a bit of paint over they would paint the next door neighbour's as well. They'd all get out on the squares and throw flags up on the washing poles from the top pipes so that every block was decorated. Every flat block would build altars to the Sacred Heart and we'd have a lovely procession going through the flats. Then we'd have a Mass in the evening. That's all gone now. They haven't done it for years. It used to bring the neighbours together. There was great excitement. All the kids would be real excited when the place was being painted and the flags were being thrown. Everybody would be looking for a veil and wreath, or a bit of curtain or anything for the parade. It was for the kids.

The Liffey was a focal point for anyone living along the quays. In the summer, all the fellas would swim in the Liffey. On a good day you'd see them on the steps, stripped off, with crowds around Queen's Street Bridge watching them. That's gone too. You can't swim in the Liffey any more. You'd also see the fellas fishing on the Liffey. They all had rods at certain times of the year, and they'd catch fish and eels. I don't think there are any fish in it now.

I also remember the women in the flats went out to Dollymount to collect cockles, mussels and winkles. Then they'd sell them in big tin basins, at the gate, to passers by and the kids. I remember my great grandmother saying, 'Don't be going up there to that oul wan. They're filthy.' But you'd go up anyway, with your safety pin, and eat a feed of them. On a good summer's day the neighbours would head off to the sea and they'd bring back piles of cockles and give them to the old people.

I can barely remember boats on the Liffey. I think they were going out in my day. But I do remember swans. It was lovely to watch them and they always went down in pairs. It's years and years since I've seen swans on the Liffey. It was much cleaner then. You could look right down through the water, at the fish. I remember seeing them myself. When the tide was out you'd see the old junk people had thrown in starting to pile up. The smell got worse as the years went by.

The part of the Liffey that goes through the city doesn't have any meaning for the people who live along it anymore. But when I was young, and even before my time, it was a very important part of life in the centre of the city.

My memories of the quays have always been of run down buildings and derelict sites, but having lived with my grandparents and having constantly asked them questions about Dublin and how it was when they were young, it had an air of grandeur. There was great life there, a lot of families lived in the houses along the quays. They were teeming with life.

There was a bit of industry as well. In between the houses there was a courtyard into the back. They all had a yard and there was always some kind of a little factory or workshop going. It gave a little employment. My own great-grandfather and his brothers had a forge somewhere along there. That's all gone now.

I remember saying to my uncles and my mother when I was elected to the corporation, the one ambition that I have is to get the quays restored and see people living there again. When I was growing up, and we had the shop in Meath Street, a lot of people remembered my family from living on the quays. It always impressed me when they would say to my mother and the Foleys, 'Weren't they great times on the quays. Hadn't we great times there? Weren't they smashing places to live? It'll never be the same again. Dublin'll never be the same again. They are only traffic lanes now. And once all life centred around there. Look at the quays now, they're devastated.'

I didn't go to the Feeno (Phoenix Picture House) or the Tivo (Tivoli). Everybody else went, my mother, and my uncles, so I heard about them. The Feeno was across the quay from us. I think it was closed down when I was small. But I heard all the stories. There's nothing there now. Absolutely nothing.

I went to school in George's Hill. A lot of the pupils there were quay people. My mother had gone to it and her mother before her. This was because they lived across from it. It was the centre of Dublin and I think it's an awful pity that no one lives there now. Dublin started on the water and our first settlements were there. The Liffey was an amenity area, always was, even when I was a child. Now it's not even noticed.

When we were talking about the development of all the new roads for Dublin Corporation it reminded me of the time I had been to Amsterdam and I felt it was very like Dublin. For instance, we call the inner city of Dublin north and south, the area between the canals and the Liffey. In Amsterdam you have the same kind of situation. You have the main central canal and then you have the outer canals. And that's their inner city. In that section of Amsterdam you are not allowed touch any of the buildings unless you're restoring them. You can't widen roads. No cars are allowed in the centre. They're allowed to park along the canals but they can't be driven any further. All the rest of the lanes and roads are as they were hundreds of years ago. Some are only eight foot and ten foot wide. They're walkways. Everything is very central once you get to the canal, just like here.

But they *use* their waterways and canals. Everybody uses little boats, visitors as well as the people who live in Amsterdam. It's the quickest, most economical and efficient way of getting from one end of the city to the other. It's also the most scenic. You're passing through Amsterdam's history and they give you a history of almost all the houses you're passing. You can see the architecture from the different periods in time. I'd like to see Dublin like that. We should develop the canals and the Liffey, because they're a beautiful amenity, and preserve the area between the inner city.

The Board of Works is responsible for the canals and the corporation does its best to clean them up. I remember a couple of months ago getting on to the Minister for Fisheries about what I thought was scum on the top of the canal. It was so thick that when people threw in plastic containers it was sticking on them. So I asked him if he could clear it off. He told me that they couldn't because the scum is algae, necessary for the life of the canal. They have to leave it there. To me it looked like sticky dirty stuff.

You'd be poisoned if you fell into the canals in Amsterdam but the surface is clean. The sides and the banks are also kept very clean but you couldn't fall in without getting some kind of dreadful disease, so nobody swims in them.

When I was younger people walked everywhere. In the evening when we were very small, my mother would get the high pram and the baby would be put into it. We'd be put sitting on top. We'd go into town and have a walk around the shop windows at night. It was a great pastime. All the women used to do it. They wouldn't go into a pub or a restaurant or a coffee shop. They'd just go walking, all around George's Street, Grafton Street. Maybe another night they'd go down Henry Street or Earl Street. No such thing as that now. All the shops are shuttered.

There was a bit more to do at night. There were the theatres and the variety shows. They were all over the place. We were brought down to St Anthony's Hall as kids by my uncles. Every Sunday night there was a variety show. But that isn't there anymore.

There was great entertainment in Dublin years ago and tons of local talent. I still believe that it's there but it has no outlet. Television has changed that. It's so easy to switch on Sunday Night in the Olympia, as opposed to going to the Olympia. You went to the shows then, they were very cheap.

Fr Matthew's Hall had shows and there'd be pantomimes at St Anthony's Hall, and at other local venues such as Guinness's Hall. Guinness's still have a show there but it's mostly for their workers and their families. Sometimes local groups will go in and put on a show. There are all kinds of little groups in the Liberties. The children are very talented.

My mother told me when she was young she was brought out to the Phoenix Park with the dogs and my grandfather or an uncle would put her standing in the middle of an open space. She was tiny, she still is, and they'd say to her, 'Now stay there and don't move whatever you do.' They'd lead the dogs off hundreds of yards away, let them off the leash and they'd run straight for my mother. They'd almost be touching her when they'd divide around her. It seemed a strange way to train the dogs. She was terrified but as soon as their noses would almost get to her chest, they'd divide and go around her.

My mother's uncles had a boxing club on the quays, St Francis Boxing Club. Anyone who was interested in boxing would go there and they'd get their training. They were professional boxers but they loved the sport so much that they enjoyed the young fellas coming in and training. Eamonn Andrews began his boxing career in St Francis Club. My uncles trained him. He used to call up to the house for the key of the Club, all the fellas did. They'd go down and start training on their own and then my uncles would follow.

I am trying to get a boxing club going and there's a great tradition of greyhound racing. Lots of people used to keep dogs in the back of their houses. My grandparents always kept dogs and this helped to create a great atmosphere in the Liberties.

My uncles organised a race as well. It was called the Wooden Cup Race. The runners would come from all over and they'd run up the quays to the Phoenix Park and then down the other side of the quays. The prize was a wooden cup which they had carved themselves. But there were lots of other prizes, hams and turkeys and things like that. It was a well known race at the time. I never knew of that race until I was organising The Liberties Around the Houses Race. People used to say to me, 'Sure it's no wonder you're like that, it's in your family.'

The Liberties race started six years ago. It's quite an event, the biggest race of its kind here and in Britain. It's on the last Thursday in May, every year. It is in and around the same time as the Liberties Festival. It's always an evening race. It's a nice time of the year and it brings a great atmosphere to the centre of the Liberties.

Sport and the Liberties have always gone hand in hand. The area was always very well known for its boxers. It just seemed that the people who lived there were attracted to that sport. The National Stadium wasn't too far away on the South Circular Road and an evening there is a brilliant night's entertainment. The Dublin wit flies. It's unbelievable. You'll hear sayings that you never heard before. I love it. There's a magic atmosphere about the National Stadium. I believe it is going to be moved into the National Sports Centre which will be based on the northside. It's been with us for so long. I wouldn't like to see it being shifted.

My wishes for Dublin in the future are to see the quays built up, and to see people living along them. I want to see shops and apartments and a couple of hotels right down along. I'd like to see the quays developed from Heuston Station, down to the docks. I want to see more and better inner city housing with people living back in Dublin over the shops as they did years ago. There are too many empty shells over shops. I'd like to see shopkeepers develop them and perhaps receive a grant or tax relief to do it.

I'd like to see the DART extended to Tallaght, Clondalkin and Blanchardstown. It should be connected to Heuston Station and Tara Street. The same on the northside into Amiens Street. This way people would have a good transport system into the centre of the city.

I'd like the corporation to modify their road plans. I realise that most of the road plans have been going on for thirty years and are past certain stages of development. In Parnell Street they've already gone ahead with the road plan, so there's no turning back. But I'd like to see them modify the plans for places like Clanbrassil Street. There you'll have a 48ft road and two 10ft footpaths with houses and shops on the western side.

I'd like to see everybody with a decent standard of living, good housing, good education, plenty to eat, plenty to drink and enough for entertainment. I'd like to see people returning to the better value of life that was there when I was younger, having more respect for the elderly and the neighbours and looking out more for them. Not to be so greedy, avaricious as it seems a lot have become. I want to see safer neighbourhoods and if there is a value set on life they will be safe and the elderly will be looked after.

It's an awful pity the corporation went ahead and built Tallaght and Clondalkin in the way they did. They're just a wilderness of houses. They have no centres, there's no sense of township about them. If they'd built the schemes on a smaller scale, differently designed from one another, if they'd given each small scheme its own centre, the quality of life would have been improved. To put people out into the wilderness, no town centre, no amenities, no adequate schooling, not enough churches is one of the biggest crimes that Dublin Corporation ever committed. I deal daily with people who were put out to Tallaght and it's breaking their hearts. All they want is to get back into the city centre.

We should improve the flats that we have had for the last forty or fifty years; build on the derelict sites. The good thing is that we now have a refurbishment scheme, it hasn't started yet but it will begin in the spring, and Oliver Bond, Marrowbone Lane and Fatima Mansions will be refurbished from top to bottom.

I think at last the message has got through. What will happen is that old kitchens will be removed and completely fitted out. New showers and bathrooms will go in. They'll be replastered and rewired and painted from top to bottom. People will be able to choose from ten different colour schemes. One flat in each scheme will be turned over to a show flat. That way people can pick and choose what they want. They will be able to have central heating if they want it. Some people would prefer to keep their fires. The corporation will take down or add walls where necessary. Perhaps some will want an extra bedroom or a bigger living area. The outside brickwork will be repointed and the general area outside will be landscaped, replanted. The entrances will be changed, there will be more than one main entrance. For the people on the ground floor their entrances will be privatised, with little walls in front to give them more a feeling of their own private property. This will all help the quality of life.

Mary Black

Daddy comes from Rathlin Island and when he came to Dublin he didn't know anybody at all. He just hopped on a bus from town, didn't know where it was bringing him and said to the bus conductor, 'Will you bring me to some place where I can find digs?' The fellow left him off at Kelly's Corner and directed him across to Charlemont Street and that's how we all started in Charlemont Street. He got a room in digs for a while. A few years later he met Mammy, who is a Dubliner, and they just started in a room in a tenement house and as the children were born they would take on another room. He ended up buying the house after he was in it for about twenty or twenty-five years. It took him that long to get the money to buy it.

We had a shop there and my mother used to work in it. People used to come in and sort of confide in her and talk about their different problems.

Charlemont Street was more like a playground to us. The backyards of the houses were just literally yards. There were long strips of clothes on lines and no place to run, so we used to end up playing on the street. When I think back, and it's not that long ago, between twenty and twenty-five years, we used to be swinging on the lampposts and dashing across the road. You'd be murdered now if you did that, killed by a bus or a truck. The difference in the traffic alone is just unbelievable.

There was what we called The Lawn, a big sort of wasteland at the back of Earlsfort Terrace and around the back of Adelaide Road and Harcourt Street. It ran right around the back of all the gardens of the big old houses. There were orchards there. We used to rob orchards, as all kids do. We used to look over this wall that was the back of a house on Harcourt Terrace and whose was it, but Michael McLiammoir's and Hilton Edward's. I often remember on a summer evening you would see them sitting out with their straw hats in the garden, sipping tea or drinking cocktails. We used to all sit peering over the wall. They didn't mean anything to us, they were just rich people. I didn't know who the hell they were. We used to see them walking up and down Charlemont Street, especially Michael, and you would always know he was coming because you would get the smell first. He always had this very strong, perfumed aftershave, a spicy smell. It was lovely, and he always held his head really high. We had a kind of respect for him. He definitely had a presence, that even the children were aware of.

I remember him catching me robbing his orchard. One day we thought there was nobody in the house and the other kids slipped me over the wall. I was the lightest, and I had to run over and pick up the apples, the ones that had fallen on the ground. Next thing didn't he come running out and just as I was getting to the wall he caught me. He gave out and said he was going to bring us round to the police, but he didn't. He said I was not to be coming in over the wall. I'll never forget the fright I got. I don't think I ever got into a garden to rob an orchard again. He was just one of the characters.

I suppose having a shop you came across them more than the average person. A fella used to come in called Christy, I don't know what his surname was, we just knew him as Christy. He came in every morning for his half pint of milk, the little triangular ones. When, at certain times, his behaviour changed, my mother always knew there was going to be a full moon. There was this picture on the wall, it was a cat advertising coal or something and he'd walk straight in and have a conversation with the cat. He had a name on the cat and all. On these particular mornings my mammy said, 'It's going to be a full moon tonight, Christy's gone a bit . . .' He was always very gentle, a lovely man, but he would go completely loopy at that time and as soon as the full moon would pass he'd be back, quite normal again. So there is certainly something to be said about the full moon, it was so obvious, it really was.

My mammy would have loads of stories to tell about the different characters. There was one woman in the street, Emily was her name, and she was a little bit simple. She used to go around and do all the messages for the old people. She was middle-aged when we were young. She had a great way with the younger kids and always sang to them. When Sé, my oldest brother, was born my mother used to have him sitting out in the pram and as soon as he'd see Emily coming he'd start to sing Daisy or whatever she was singing. He was only about nine or ten months old and my mother used to say the talent was coming out even then. Before he was one year old he could sing four songs. Everybody knew and everybody loved her. All the kids used to chase her and slag her and she'd come running after us and we used to think it was great fun. There were lots and lots of characters, that's what I liked about Dublin. No matter where you went there was some character or another. Even now it's still quite obvious, people are very much themselves.

St Ultan's Hospital was at the top of our street and my mother often had to run up there with a very sick child. There were other hospitals around, Harcourt Street was one, but St Ultan's was for the poorer people who couldn't afford to pay for their kids. In those days you would have to be very ill before you went to a doctor, not like nowadays the way people run to the doctor for anything. I remember one time, myself and my brother Michael, were playing 'house' with this older girl and we sat down to a makey up dinner. It was muck and plants and what have you and we ate the whole bowl of gunge. That night we woke up and we were pukin' up black stuff. My mother didn't know what we had eaten and she ran, with one under each arm, up to St Ultan's and we were kept in for two weeks. I think having the hospital there, so close, was really an advantage.

Mammy had it hard when we were young. Luckily Daddy wasn't often out of

work but still it was hard trying to make ends meet.

Another time when my younger brother Martin was a baby, he was very ill. He had a murmur in his heart. He took very bad and got pneumonia and was hospitalised. My mother didn't see him for four months. There was some sort of virus going round and they wouldn't let her in. She used to go to the door and see the matron and the matron would say, 'He's a little better today,' and she'd have to be content with that and go home. He took very bad one day and she was sent for. He was really on his last breath. The nurses were saying, 'Well it doesn't look very good.' They were really saying there was little or no hope for him. He was there around five months at this stage. The nurse who was on duty said, 'They don't believe in this in this hospital,' and she took out a jar of Vick and she rubbed it all around his chest, under his arms and everywhere. Within minutes, my mother said, it was like a miracle. They were praying over him as well and the next thing he starts to breathe easier and after that he never looked back. The nurse and the Vick saved his life. It's strange how people believe in these things. There might be something in it, I don't really know, but I just think it's really funny.

We weren't allowed to cross the road. We would have to be brought by somebody. Only very occasionally would we go into town. At Christmas we'd go down to Pim's in George's Street and that was as far as we would go. Going to O'Connell Street was a major sort of expedition. George's Street was a really big street in those days, it was as busy as Henry Street would be nowadays. We'd go into Pim's and see Santa Claus, go over as far as Thomas Street, where Mammy would do a good deal of her shopping. Once a year Daddy's relations would come and they would bring us into town, to a film or something and that was unbelievable. We never had a car. To get into a car was such a treat. My kids now are used to the car and when they get into a bus they are all excited and delighted. I just laugh because it was the complete opposite for us. To get into a car in my day you were really doing the rich kid bit.

I remember one particular incident, it was Hallowe'en. A friend and myself were all dressed up. We were about nine or ten and we actually ventured way down as far as Camden Street collecting for the Hallowe'en party. She was real brazen and I just followed behind. We even went into pubs and we made a fortune. She stood up and sang, *I want to be Bobby's Girl*, I remember it well. My song was, *Puc ar Buile*, and the two of us would sing our party piece. All the men up at the bar thought it was hilarious. We came back with our pockets full of money, laden down and, of course, to this day I never told my mother where I was. I just said we were going around the houses and we sang and everyone gave us money.

Having the country background had another advantage. Come the summer holidays we were shipped off to Rathlin Island for six weeks. It was fabulous to leave a place like the heart of the city and to go off up to Rathlin and run wild in the fields. An awful lot of the children from the city would have hardly ever seen a cow and I really think we had the best of both worlds. We were real city kids but we also had the advantage of going off for the summer, something we used to live for. On Rathlin we'd go down to the oul' hall and there'd be a *ceili* on and it would be great. It was very rural, no electricity, no running water. They were even more behind than other rural areas because it was an island. To us it was heaven. I remember bringing home presents to the kids in the street. You'd bring home a big bag of sweets, it being northern Ireland the sweets were different; the penny sweets would be different from the penny sweets at home. That made all the difference, getting something that you never got before, even though basically it was probably a penny toffee, the same as you got in your own shop, just wrapped differently. There was always great excitement when we were coming home, because the kids knew we were coming and we would spend about one and sixpence on a whole load of penny sweets. It was a great feeling.

Mammy was a singer herself and she had an interest in music and Daddy was very involved in music, but on the traditional side of things. We were different to the other children in that we had that traditional background. Daddy used to play the fiddle and the mandolin. There were always instruments lying around the house and the boys, especially, used to pick up the instruments and knock out a few tunes or copy and listen and play. We all had a good musical ear.

We got on well with everyone, but I always felt a bit different, I think, because of my father's input into the family. Daddy used to invite his own friends for music evenings in the house. The locals would rarely join us. There wasn't really much music in and around the street, except maybe at Christmas when people wanted a good hooley and everybody would sing, but you wouldn't really come across people playing instruments. People didn't seem to play music unless they came from a traditional background or were in a dance band, a big band perhaps playing modern music, but I rarely came across anyone.

I used to do Irish dancing and I can often remember waiting for my daddy to come in with the one and sixpence. He might be late and my mammy would say he'd be here in a minute. She would not have it to give to me. My mother loved Irish dancing but she never really got a chance to do it because her mother couldn't afford Irish dancing classes either. Her story was that in her youth, when all the kids were going to the Irish dancing, she'd follow and look through the keyhole and learn all the steps that way. When the others came out some of them would say, 'Oh I can't remember that step,' and my mother would say, 'It's this way.' She was a brilliant Irish dancer and still remembers all the different steps, hornpipe and all. So she always wanted us, naturally, to have things she could never have. I was very good at the Irish dancing and won thirteen or fourteen medals for it.

I went to St Louis School in Rathmines and they were great for music and singing. In retrospect I think they had a great influence on my career. They used to put us in for the Feis Ceoil.

I was in the Young Dublin Singers. Twink would have been in it as well, and Maxi. There are a good lot of people in the music business now who were in that school. It played a big part in bringing out the music in people. We even made a record and we opened or launched the Eddie Delaney fountain in Dame Street. I can remember standing in the slush singing and it was lashing rain down on top of us.

My mother is terrified of water and we were never allowed up the canal unless she was with us. We used to go pinkeen fishing and that sort of thing, but the canal was basically a no go area. She thought we were going to drown up there. She wouldn't put her toe in water; she'd be smothering if she saw someone in swimming. I remember the barges. You rarely see one now, but in those days it was a normal occurrence to see the locks filling up and the barges going through. We would stand on the edge watching the people on the boat having a chat. It was great. Another thing I remember is that outside the pub up the road there was always a horse and cart, and the horse eating out of the bag. We'd end up playing with the horses outside the pub. Not that long ago it would be quite normal for your milk to be delivered by horse and cart. You rarely see them now, except perhaps the odd horse and cart with scrap metal.

There was one family in the street with triplets, aged about three or four. One day they found their way up to the canal and the two boys fell in. The little girl grabbed onto one of them by the hair and held onto him until help came, but they lost the other little fellow. It was a very sad case. A lot of children were lost in that canal, and I remember seeing a woman being dragged out. It's a very frightening thing for a child to see. I didn't know what was happening. I saw a crowd gathering as I was on my way back to school and I saw her dead body. I'll never forget the colour. I suppose that is partly why my mother was wary of it.

I think the Millennium will give the people of Dublin a feeling of pride for their city. Generally speaking things will be done. How much, remains to be seen, but we'll see at the end of the year exactly how much has been done.

They have ruined the city in a lot of ways. I remember when I was in my teens how amazed I was to see all the houses down to Adelaide Road and Earlsfort Terrace without roofs. The developers came in and took the roofs off the lovely Georgian houses so they would rot and they would get the right to pull them down as dangerous buildings. I think it was dreadful to see them getting away with that. It's only now, when it's nearly too late, that they are beginning to realise that they have to start looking at the city as an old city and try to preserve the old buildings. Far too many beautiful old buildings have been knocked down and it's a shame because it's a fabulous city. It has so much to offer.

I think they are beginning to cop on at long last. I think the inner city rebuilding of houses has been an incredible step towards keeping the city alive. There has been a big question mark about our own street for years. Going back twenty years, I remember my father saying those houses will be down in five years and most of them are still sitting there. Some of them are gone, it's like someone with a bad set of teeth. There are props holding up my father's house and the house beside his is falling down. Then there is a house standing on its own two doors down. My brother still has the shop open there, it's a bicycle shop now. When my parents had it it used to be a grocery shop with coal and you name it. My mother used to be weighing up stones of coal. They had to work very hard to make any sort of a living at all.

The street as it stands now is a bit of an eye sore really. They have widened it at the top and it's almost modern, then further down the street it has all these fallen down houses. It's as if they don't know what they are doing with it. Eventually I think what they hope to do is to widen the road and link it up completely with Harcourt Street and make it a straight run through. It's a problem with traffic. At Kelly's Corner there's a triangle thing you have to go round. I really don't know what is going to happen. Some of those houses are quite dangerous. They have been there for years. The shop is still open and with all the flats there is a good community spirit in Charlemont Street, which is great to see. On the far side of the street, where they built the flats, they have built their own community hall. The people are very involved in all sorts of things and there is plenty of activity. A lot of the old people are still living there, having moved into the flats from the houses. They have also built the new red bricked corporation houses, all around the back of our houses. It's still very much alive, and even if they do knock down the old houses there will still be plenty of spirit left. It's just changing, that's all.

I wouldn't live anywhere else and I've travelled quite a bit in America and I've even been to Australia which I liked an awful lot. I'm lucky really that I don't have to live anywhere else. I'd be very, very unhappy if I had to leave Dublin. My roots are here and my family is here. Even apart from that it's just a great city, it has a lot of character and good vibes.

Joni Crone

The biggest change that I have seen is the break up of communities in the inner city. We wouldn't have called it the inner city. Macken Street was a back street. When our family moved out to Finglas in 1965 there was a total change. In Macken Street everybody knew everybody. You were practically related to people, you might as well have been as you knew everything about their families for generations.

My mother's parents lived with her when she was growing up. When I was a baby there was a family downstairs. There were two families in the one house. In the house next door to us there were two, nearly three families you could say. And all the time I was growing up there were always two families — one family in one room. You'd never see that now. There was much more sense of community and closeness.

When we moved out to Finglas there were no street names. We didn't know anybody on the street. There were fields behind us and it was half an hour on the bus to town. It was like being out in the country, Finglas was the country.

In Macken Street, I was used to going across the road to the shops where my mother would have an account book and she'd pay her bill at the end of the week. So if we went shopping it was literally across the road to Larry's to get our tea or milk or bread. If you wanted vegetables it was to Pat's next door. You went up to the Eblana for rashers or sausages, and to Mrs Nolan for potatoes. We knew everybody and everyone knew us. These people were nearly like uncles and aunts to us.

In Finglas there were no shops. There was a van that stopped a couple of streets away. There was a shopping centre that was twenty minutes walk away. As for walking — we used to get a bus into town from Pearse Street. The distance was totally different. You'd never dream of walking into town. I'd do it now, but not then.

In Finglas we lived for the first few years with the vans coming around. Then they built a very small local shopping centre, with a pub, of course. In no time that was damaged. Broken glass everywhere. It was set fire to and now it looks like a bomb hit it. Even when it's fixed up, in no time it's gone again.

The travellers' horses were all round the place. We got up at seven o'clock in the morning when I was going to school, over on the southside, and there would be three or four horses in the garden. We'd have to shoo them out. We never had a garden in the city centre, never mind horses.

I think that the attitude of anyone who has moved out to these suburbs, and I don't only mean Finglas, is very different. There was more a sense of caring and knowing, a pride in the area, a community spirit in the inner city. The first time we saw the likes of shops being set on fire we thought the revolution was upon us, things were falling apart. Then it just became a regular thing. There are shutters and barriers up everywhere. There's less of a sense of people knowing each other and more a sense of people being out for themselves, being more competitive, more protective. There's much more violence, much more crime.

My father has collected the pools for years. He'd do it when he did the church collection. Nothing ever happened to him. When we moved out to Finglas things did happen to him, young fellas would go after him on his bicycle. It just shows the changes that have taken place.

My mother was born in Macken Street. Apparently, she walked home from Holles Street Hospital to Macken Street, two days after I was born. She was born and reared there and lived there all her life. Her mother was born in Winetavern Street and her father in Erne Street, where he lived all his life. Those two streets are very near each other. There have been huge changes in that area.

Down the lane from us there was the Saw Mills. Up at the top at Grand Canal Street was Sir Patrick Dun's Hospital. There was Smyly's, the Protestant Boys' Home just a little bit up from that. There seemed to be lots more houses. They've built flats there now and condemned our block, knocked down our houses. My mother used to be very proud of our house because apparently de Valera was billetted there in 1916 and they put a plaque on Bolands Mills opposite it in 1966, but sure, it was gone by then. When Patrick Dun's closed I just felt, even though we weren't living there anymore, that it was the final death blow.

I wasn't supposed to play near the canal, but my uncle lived with us and he would take us for walks there. We'd go fishing for pinkeens. I used to love that but I wasn't allowed do that on my own. You'd be liable to meet Johnny Forty Coats or some oul character. You weren't allowed go down there because something might happen to you, but I was never told that there was anything sexual in it. We weren't to talk to strangers and we weren't allowed play beyond our own lane and Macken Street. So Pearse Street and Grand Canal Street seemed miles away.

There was a Bridge that used to open where you went down Macken Street towards Ringsend. I suppose it was to let the boats come up the Basin. There was a great thrill to see that go up. When that went Macken Street was just like any other road.

The houses that we had are all gone, now there are blocks of flats. The Gas Company was there and, I think, a foundry. My grandfather worked in the Gas Company and my uncle on the docks. That was another thing — people worked locally then. Now they have the new IDA building, which is very nicely designed, but the whole look of the place is changed.

On Pearse Street they have a new lot of houses, the red bricked ones. They should have done that years ago. We used to call it the Everglades, when the

Everglades was on the telly. Just waste ground. They could have built houses there instead of building blocks of flats. That way, they could have kept the community together, but they didn't.

The standard of living now, that's something I think has changed enormously. There was one sink in our kitchen, with one cold tap and one cold tap out in the yard. That was it. There was no bathroom. The toilet was outside, down the end of the garden. I didn't have a bath until I was twelve. I mean I didn't use a bathroom until we moved out to Finglas, and that was total, utter luxury and I mean it.

When I was a kid you were rich if you had a car, because nobody on my street or anywhere around had a car. On Saturday afternoons, the rich people with the cars, who were going to Lansdowne Road would park on Macken Street and we used to go out on these afternoons with our rags and our mothers' polish, and clean the hub caps and polish the cars and say, 'Mister give us a tanner, give us a half crown'. It was always a 'Mister' of course.

Sometimes you'd go out with a bucket of water and you'd clean it whether they wanted it or not. They'd come back and you'd be standing by the car and some of them would tell you to go and shite and some would give you sixpence. If you got a half crown that was brilliant. It was a great way of earning a few bob on a Saturday at the Rugby International.

My memory of the Protestant kids in Smyly's is of their short grey trousers and their little grey caps when they used to walk out. Now where they went I don't know, but you'd see them walking along the top of Grand Canal Street, marching along in file. That's the only time you'd see them, coming in and going out of the school. There was no mixing with any of the local children at all. We didn't even walk on that side of the street. We walked on the other side. Imagine not even walking on the same side of the street. To this day when I'm walking down that street, I automatically cross over to 'our' side of the road. There were no shops on the other side anyway. Only Burke's Pub. So you wouldn't have any reason to be there.

I remember when my eldest brother got married, he married a non Catholic. His marriage to someone who wasn't baptised was a total and utter disgrace. She wasn't even a Protestant. When Thomas got married and brought home this non Catholic, this exotic creature from London, my mother got his best friend, who was an electrician, to put an electric light out in the toilet. Everybody thought we were real posh because we had a light in our toilet. Who did we think we were? We had the switch in the kitchen so you put it on there before you went out. This was luxury . . . One of my jobs was to cut up newspapers for toilet paper and hang them on the nail. The idea of buying toilet paper would have been considered too much of a luxury. The things people take for granted now like hot water and a bathroom, were considered luxuries then. This has changed, thankfully.

When we were kids we used to go to the Palace, now the Academy, on a Saturday. It used to be called the Embassy, officially, but we called it the Palace. That was in Pearse Street and we walked to it. A long walk, we thought. It was sixpence downstairs and ninepence upstairs, old money, and then it changed to ninepence downstairs and a shilling upstairs. This rise was a tragedy. It was such a huge difference for us.

In town there was the Capitol and the Metropole, both of which are gone, and the Adelphi. They were the ones we would go to the most. I don't know why we thought the Savoy was a cut above the rest. Somehow you couldn't go there unless you were dressed up to the nines.

I remember going to the Capitol, way up to the top, and again, the cheap seats. You'd never get that now. We'd go to the Royal. My mother was a Royalette. My father and she met when he was playing for Queen's Park Football Club. That's gone as well. So we went to the Royal and the old Abbey. My mother's father was great for going to the theatre and even went to the opera on occasion. He was very unusual though. Round our way all we ever did was go to the pictures, or the Royal. That was about it.

One of the biggest events that I remember as a kid was when Cardinal Agaganian came to visit. The idea of the Pope coming to visit would have been science fiction. But the Cardinal was coming to visit and the cavalcade was due along the top of Macken Street. My mother used to sew a lot like most of the women around then. She had her own machine, and used to cut up her clothes and make smaller clothes for all of us. We hardly ever bought anything when we were kids. She made everything.

All the mothers were up sewing half the night doing flags and bunting to go across the top of our street. There were weeks and weeks of doing this. It seemed to go on for ever. I remember my mother doing a huge big banner of St Patrick and of the Virgin Mary and then she did another one with the Pope in the middle. Beautifully made, with fringing and bunting ... just for your man to go by in five seconds.

I don't even remember seeing him. He just went by in his car and that was it. This was the big event we were all waiting for.

Apart from that momentous visit, Corpus Christi was the big thing every year in our neighbourhood. We'd strew petals along the road, as the procession went round all the local streets. From Westland Row it went up our street and along Grand Canal Street.

There was one Protestant family on our street and they had a piano. We had a Jewish landlord. There was certainly an attitude that Jews were penny pinching, that Jews were mean. They were good with money but they were mean. Protestants were very definitely above you, snooty and hot potatoish in their speech and you didn't mix with them. We played with them occasionally and I remember going in to play their piano. I didn't know them well. They moved out quite early on but they did mix and that was unusual.

That has changed in Dublin. I see it now on the South Circular road. There's a much bigger ethnic mix. In the last ten years we have seen the establishment of a mosque on the South Circular Road, an Irish Islam Centre, an increase in the population of Asians from Pakistan, China and Vietnam. There are quite a number of clothes shops and newsagents that open on Saturdays and all day Sundays, they have different opening hours.

There are some things happening in Finglas and Darndale and Tallaght and Coolock with Women's Groups coming together. But we need much more of that. The issue of the 'Feminisation of Poverty' is beginning to be discussed, but only just. I think we've potential for great social change, with much more thriving communities. Ballyfermot is a classic example. People are taking much more pride in their area and there's more a community sense now. These places used to be regarded as the wilderness, but this is changing.

There have been changes too in transport, with CIE breaking up into smaller companies, that's a good thing. But there needs to be a much more creative approach to transport. I'm not sure if this is nostalgia or not, but I seem to remember as a child, bus conductors being very helpful to women with kids and prams and jamming things in and finding space for them. Now it seems that women, with children in buggies, are considered a nuisance. Buses fly past the stop half the time. The new buses have a huge step up to them and you've more steps to go up when you get into them. It seems to me that you have far less space than you had before. If only they'd go out and consult the women who use them, mothers with small children, older people, people in wheelchairs, and change the design to the users' needs.

When I was living in Finglas we lived at the terminus, thankfully, at Plunkett Avenue, so we were assured of a bus when it came. We always waited a half an hour. By the second or third stop they'd be full. There'd be droves at the other stops all the way into town. It's nothing unusual to wait an hour for a bus out in Finglas or Coolock or Ballymun or Darndale, you name it.

Most of the people would want to go to the village only. So I think if we changed the system and had more buses going out to the local village and more buses going into the centre of the city we would have a much more efficient system, that would meet the needs of the people. A system that isn't designed, up in an office, by someone who never uses a bus. This is obvious from the design of them and the way they fly around the place scaring young kids and old people.

What's most pressing for me at the moment, in Clanbrassil Street and Synge Street, is the proposed motorway. I think if we had more links between the working class people in Clanbrassil Street, along the South Circular Road, in Finglas and in Ballymun, it would be easier to put pressure on county councils. If we had more interaction and supported each other, because we share the same issues, we would have more success.

Another thing is the planning. We've had no planning in this city. The so called planners have made a mess of the city and the suburbs. We've had nothing but housing estates, houses, houses, houses and no consideration for amenities like schools or hospitals. Where I was living in Macken Street you could walk to your hospital or your church, you could walk to your shops. You could literally walk anywhere in fifteen minutes. Now you have people isolated. No facilities, no amenities, no landscaping. You might as well put people into barracks. There's no long term planning at all. Our city has been devastated.

Look what they've done. It's as though they see fields and they just build houses. They don't think anything about what it means to live in a place. But the kind of changes I'm talking about are changes through communities, and having a sense of your area. This is happening. Down in Pearse Street, for example, there's a place called St Andrew's, an old school that my brother went to. That has a day care centre which has a place for the elderly and a youth group. It has training courses. That's hopeful and it is not controlled by the church either.

I would see hope in the new houses that are being built in the inner city, now, and that's twenty years later. We moved out in 1965, it's now 1988. It's taken twenty years. Hopefully in the next twenty, people will take more of a responsibility and insist, as they have in the Liberties, that they're not moving. Insist on what they want.

Elizabeth Geraghty

I was born in the Rotunda where practically all Dublin people were born and we lived on City Quay until 1916. During the Rising, when the IRA brought the boat up the Liffey to attack Liberty Hall, the heavy bombing shook the house we lived in, the top of it split open and it became unsafe.

My mother had to look around for somewhere else for us to live because we became nervous of staying in the house, although other tenants were in it. My mother's cousin who lived in Marlborough Street said there were two small rooms in Marlborough Place empty. We had big old fashioned furniture, big old fashioned sideboard and brass beds, the usual at the time. When she went to look at them we found that we wouldn't have been able to get into the place with all the stuff. But in the emergency we simply had to take the two rooms.

At this stage, just after the Rebellion, the lads were all deported. Andy and Jack were in Frongoch, my brother Paddy was in a prison just outside of Manchester. Between one thing and another the furniture was just packed into these two small rooms, because there was only myself and my mother, until such times as she could get a bigger place.

Eventually we got two basement rooms in a big old fashioned Georgian house. There was the kitchen, with a big double range, with what would be a maid's room off it and then a back kitchen. It was right behind the Gresham Hotel.

The people who owned the house were named Morgan and they owned a dairy right beside us. The house was fairly nice and the tenants were very nice, but as it was just after 1916 the women there were all married to soldiers and sailors. And of course we were Republican so I had a tough time as a youngster. Even my mother didn't know how hard a time I was getting.

After the 1916 Rebellion was over they struck a little enamel button with all the heads of the 1916 men on it. I had one of those on my coat and I got bashed by all the ex-soldiers' youngsters. I wouldn't go to school in Gardiner Street so I went back to my old school in Townsend Street.

It was that time when they were calling the Sinn Féin 'chimney pot fighters' and 'under the bed fighters.' They called them all sorts of names and I had to survive. There was only my mother till the lads started coming out of prison. Then the next two rooms became idle and my mother took them for the lads coming home. That was coming up to Christmas. I'm not sure if it was September or October when the first of them arrived. I know they were all home for that Christmas in 1916.

After the coal strike, all the men on the docks were involved in the 1913 strike, this Jew by the name of Cohen, set up what was known as the Diamond Coal Company. He recognised the Union immediately. I wouldn't know if there were any other Jews who did the same but he recognised the Union and he wasn't involved in the 1913 strike. My father, being one of the men involved in the strike, got very great with Louis Cohen and his two brothers.

They had a song composed for Cohen Coal Merchant in D'Olier Street and the words went something like:

'Hurrah Hurrah Hurrah Hurray
And where would you see such a name on a dray
As Moses ri-tourali-ourali-ay'

Louis Cohen had a big house down in Kenilworth Square. Mrs. Cohen had very broken English, she spoke Yiddish, and his daughter's name was Betty. He was talking to my mother and she probably told him about me leaving school. He asked would I go and take up a job in the house in Kenilworth Square. Now I'd have only just past fourteen years, but you thought you'd never get to fourteen in my day until you'd get out to get some money. There was no money. During 1916 I saw my mother putting an onion on the fire and sitting down and eating bread and salt with it. That was with the skin and everything. We were very poor, but we can't claim the prerogative on that because everyone else was in the same boat as ourselves.

I got the job in Kenilworth Square with Mr Cohen and Betty, but never having been away from home I was very unhappy. When I fixed the fire the old lady used to come and if I'd put in a piece of paper wrong she'd take it out. I couldn't communicate with her because of her broken English.

That was one reason I was very upset. The other was that the Jews have a different vessel for all the washing, the washing up after the dinner, clothes etc. Sometimes I'd take a chance when no one was looking and wash up in the nearest one to me to make it easy for myself. Along would come the lassie behind me and the next thing is I'd get pushed. There was only her and me in the house all day.

I couldn't stick it after being there for about five or six months. I got on with the daughter alright and there was another married girl. She lived a couple of doors away and her husband was one of two brothers who owned a picture house in Camden Street. I probably wouldn't have stayed that long except I got free passes to the De Luxe and, of course, I'd bring some pals along so I had that advantage. It meant a lot.

What put the kybosh on me leaving Cohen's was they had a basket on the landing for putting laundry things in. I'd put everything into it except the dish cloths. That was because at home we used to rinse out the cloth after we had washed up. My mother did that and I still do it. But they didn't. They shoved everything into the basket and then you put the basket out front and it'd be taken away by the laundry boy. One day they discovered I was not putting the dish cloths out for laundry and there was a ferocious row. When I got out to go to mass one Sunday I went home and told my mother I wasn't going back any more. She asked me why and I told her it was the food.

A couple of days after, Mr Cohen went to my mother and sat a while and my mother told him I didn't like the food. He said, 'The food shouldn't have been any reason for leaving because there is a little shop on the corner and she could leave word there and she could get what she wanted.'

But nothing would induce me to go back. I said, 'No, I'm never going there again.' The maid was called Chicksie. Between hopping and trotting I said I wouldn't have that anymore. So I got a job with a policeman.

He lived on Pleasant Street in lodgings and his name was Carroll. He became a big shot in the police afterwards. I want to emphasise that. But at that time he was only on traffic duty on Camden Street. I was minding their kids.

Then I got talking to a girl who worked in Jacob's and she said to me, 'Why don't you try Jacob's?' Now at that time Guinness's was the big job for the men and, of course, Jacob's was for women.

In those days in the drapery trade the girls would have to pay to be taken on, twenty or thirty pounds, and they got their wages back at about five shillings a week. In Cassidy's, Metcalfe's, Arnott's, all these big places, nearly all the girls lived in. It was the same as the grocery trade and the publican's, the young men nearly all lived in. It was well known which of them were good houses.

You got to know if O'Meara's on the quays was a good house or Bowe's of Fleet Street. They got a name as good houses or bad houses. That was to do with the food and how they fed the assistants.

Those lads lived in and at 8 o'clock in the morning the shop had to be opened. The cellarman had to be in to clean the place, then he went around collecting empty bottles. They sometimes got very bad food. They wouldn't shut until 10 o'clock in the evening and it might be 12 o'clock before they got to bed. Their money was very small.

The majority of the grocers' assistants weren't organised. They were completely exploited. Especially young lads coming up from the country who were after serving a couple of years in stores selling everything, beer and corn and implements.

In Merrion Square and Fitzwilliam Square all the houses were family homes when I was growing up. That was my playground around there. Doctors, solicitors, judges and all the rest lived there. They would have six or eight servants, parlour maids, house maids, cooks, kitchen maid and maybe a butler thrown in, or perhaps the chauffeur would do the butlering. At the back of the house were the coach houses or the garden where the coachman or the gardener lived with his family and the family were all servants of those people.

Wages ran to about five or six shillings a week with a half day on Wednesday. I don't ever remember them getting a half day from one o'clock on. If they got off at three or four in the afternoon they were lucky. They'd come down to Nelson's Pillar and we, as youngsters, used to jeer them.

We used to call Wednesday, the day off, Dripping Day. That's what the Dublin people would say because you'd see all those crowds of girls and boys outside of Nelson's Pillar, meeting each other, maybe some from the northside and some from the southside.

The big houses had no bathrooms in them. Usually the ground floor would be a surgery or a solicitor's office. The first floor would be the sitting room, the dining room might be at the back of the ground floor. The bedrooms would be at the top and the maids had to bring up jugs and baths of water from the basement to those people. They had to get separate baths which meant that the maids had to go up and down those stairs, maybe five, six or seven times a day carrying water up to them. Not like the poor people where they made one communal bath in front of the fire. These were the terrible, appalling conditions they worked in. You'd meet them in The Green where we'd go to play and these maids and servants would be talking and telling you about their work.

After the shops had opened in the morning, if you were out at seven o'clock, you met armies, literally armies of charwomen and window cleaners all going to the big shops all around the city to clean the brasses outside and the windows.

There were messenger boys. My goodness you'd droves of them. Nearly every place had a messenger boy. All the big shops had one and they were the most exploited section of the working class when I was growing up. You worked for a big place like Arnott's or Clery's or Todd Burns and some lady would come in from Booterstown or Greystones to buy a costume or a hat and she'd select what she wanted and write: 'Deliver it to such an address.' You'd see these poor messenger boys, after having worked all day, trotting up around Ranelagh or Palmerston at about 10 o'clock at night, with a couple of hat boxes, going out as far as Greystones to deliver them. Even though the premises would have a horse and cart or a car, they had to do it.

Whatever was left over in the butchers at the end of the day would be wrapped up and given to the messenger boy or the man that had done the cleaning. The same thing happened to the unfortunate cellarman in the pubs. He might get a drink at the last minute after working all day collecting empty bottles, cleaning up and sawdusting and cleaning the toilets.

The women would come in in the morning to do the brass work and the cleaning of the offices before the staff came and they would have to go back in the evening to set the fire because there wasn't any electricity then.

The streets were teeming with those unfortunate people. But the saddest thing that I can remember, looking back, is boys of sixteen, seventeen and eighteen years of age in their bare feet in the winter pushing hand carts. The blood would be actually teeming out of the splits in their feet. They'd be pushing the handcarts piled up high with all sorts of things. It was very sad, the awful spectacle of those poor boys.

The news boys at that time couldn't sell papers on the streets unless they wore a leather arm band with a brass plaque. This had to be issued by the police. That was to show they were licensed, and if they didn't have that they were arrested. Men's wages were very small and at that time people had very big families. It was nothing to have twelve or fourteen people in one room.

In spite of all that want and deprivation people were very proud, especially in those old tenements. There used to be old ladies on Abbey Street from the YMCA, we used to call it the Bowl. They'd stop you on the street and if you were properly dressed they'd ask if you'd had your breakfast. If you hadn't they'd give you a ticket and you went to be fed.

It was a mortal sin to accept one of the food tickets, you couldn't. But poor old knockabouts, homeless men and women on the street, you'd see them all lining up down there. We called it the Bowl, I presume because they got a bowl of soup.

Then you had Smyly's home in Rath Row. They had a school and in the front was a lovely big building and the Mission was on the far side. Not all the children were orphans. Some people put their children in to be reared. They wore a uniform and they used to take them out to meet their parents in the street. Everyone knew they were Smyly's.

The school, at the back, was a public school anyone could go to it. This was my first school and I'll tell how I went to it. My mother had an interview with the nuns in Townsend Street, the Sisters of Mercy, and made arrangements for me to go to school that morning. She made arrangements with another youngster to bring me to school, as she was going to work. The youngster that brought me to Rath Row school that first day was a grand daughter of Skin-the-Goat of the Park Murders, Kitty Monassey. My mother didn't know she was attending the school. When I came back, it being my first day, I was asked all sorts of questions. I had taken a lunch to school but you were given a bun and a cup of cocoa in Rath Row. My mother couldn't understand this and probed me more. When I told her about Kitty Monassey she was very upset. So this was the first and last day I went to Rath Row Mission School.

When we went to Marlborough Street things got just a little bit better, but the lads, when they came home from the camps, got mixed up again with the movement. The 1918 election came and, of course, Sinn Féin swept the country. People who were anti-war and even some of the soldiers that came back from the war and knew what war was all about, voted Sinn Féin. It was a complete change over.

I joined the Clann na nGael scouts and my captain was Mary White. All the youngsters from around the neighbourhood joined. I was in the Mansion House when they held their meeting. Countess Markievicz and Dev and all the leaders were in the Round Room but we were in the hall collecting for the elections.

I remember an incident that night. There was a chap there by the name of Joe McGrath who lived on Parnell Street. He was a member of the Citizen Army and he fought in the Post Office. He was very much attached to Countess Markievicz, who lived in Leinster Road at the time. He had asked me would I take his concertina and mind it. When he came out with the Countess that night I gave him back the concertina and he introduced me to her. Before this I had only known her to see. We got talking and I told her my brothers and father were in the Post Office and she invited me to the house in Leinster Road, and when I went to the house Nora Connolly was staying there. I'd known her and her father, James Connolly, in Liberty Hall, because Liberty Hall was part of my playground on a Sunday morning. All the men used to stand outside on the steps and my father would bring me over to the old Northumberland Hotel. It's all changed now of course.

When I saw Nora Connolly, I was charmed because there was someone that I knew. Looking back, I think it's very sad that the Countess has been so neglected. In those early years when I got to know her, I thought her one of the most wonderful women that I ever came in contact with, for kindliness and love. She gave Nora and me the run of the house and she provided us with everything, even tickets for concerts.

I remember she wore a long cardigan with a belt, and a hat. She was a tall thin woman. She had a special tea pot and she'd make the tea and we'd sit down at a small little table between us and the fire. She'd tell us all about her childhood and

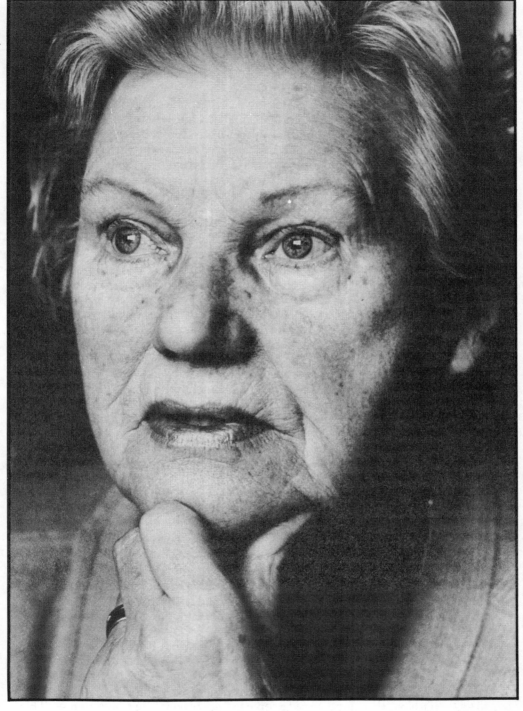

her sisters and growing up. I became what you would call a devotee, a fan. I loved her, I absolutely loved her.

Also in 1918 there was news of the Russian Revolution. I knew nothing about geography, absolutely nothing. Russia to me could have been the moon at the time, but everyone was talking about the success of the Revolution. It made you take notice, and I took notice. I'd be down at Liberty Hall discussing socialism. I look at that now as an extension of school. I was beginning to get a grasp of what was happening in the world.

There was a picture house in O'Connell Street, called the Sackville, run by a Jewish woman. It was just up from O'Connell Bridge, where the Green Rooster is now. She and her family came to England from Russia before the Revolution and settled somewhere there. They had suffered before the Revolution and she was very broad minded. She put on the first pictures of the Revolution, *Petrograd* and *Ten Days That Shook The World* and other Russian pictures. The extraordinary thing about it was that the theatre used to be full of people.

At that time, the terrible idea that the devil was behind Communism, and the religious animosity towards it wasn't there. The whole idea was new to the working class of Dublin and we thought it was a tremendous thing that had happened in a place so far away as Russia.

I started looking for books to read about it. My first one was Connolly's *Labour in Irish History*. From this I developed and became a socialist. It was like a new religion for me. There was something wrong with the conditions under which I had previously lived where people would come up in huge big carriages with chauffeurs and they couldn't even carry their own parcels. It hit me that there was something which had provoked this Revolution in Russia. From that I started reading.

I got talking to an Englishman called Bell who belonged to the British Socialist Party. He came to Ireland and I got into an argument with him. At first I was very proud because of what had happened in Russia, but after the 1918 elections when everything was Sinn Féin and, 'Break the connection with England,' I was a bit confused.

When I was young the city was like a big country village. Everybody knew everybody and you could let a young child out. That child could travel from here to Christ Church Place or Dolphin's Barn or Finglas and be safe.

That's the city I was born in and that's the city I loved. I've walked through Dublin City at three in the morning from what they called Cinderella Dances and I never had anyone say a wrong word to me. In my young days the men used to stand around the corners. They used to call them 'corner boys.' Looking back those men kept Dublin safe because if a girl or a woman or a child was molested you could call on them. They were all honest, hard working, morally decent men who had no money to go anywhere after work so they stood at corners. They weren't what you would call riff-raff, there would be one or two, as in any crowd, but the majority of them met their companions at the corner just like in the country they would meet on a bridge.

The city was perfectly safe because there was communication between us and all our local policemen. Ordinary policemen, ones who walked on the beat, would become as well known as doctors in the area. So if there was a wrong done they could nearly give you a family history, they were that close.

We didn't have this thing of old people being afraid in their own homes. They didn't have to shut their door in those days. We youngsters used to do the messages for them. I used to collect ten old age pensions, that's how I know how much they got in those days.

I remember when the Treaty was signed and when the change over took place, a terrible thing was done by Clann na nGael. They took a shilling off the old age pension. It was only six shillings and sixpence and then it was reduced to five shillings and sixpence.

With the departure of the British and pro British elements from the country, what have we got in their place? We have our own, as we call them — from Clongowes, Clonliffe, Belvedere and Blackrock Colleges — solicitors, stockbrokers, lawyers, judges, and a whole new capitalist system of our own. We can't point now to the English or any others outside of Ireland. We have Irishmen in power running the country, and what are they doing? We're back again with the same awful poverty just as it was in my day.

It appals me when I look back on their backgrounds and think of what they came from and see what they are today and how they're exerting their power to keep the unfortunate worker down. Attacking the trade unions! I can never see why anyone, be it man or woman or child, should stand up and attack a trade union. Terrible sacrifices were made to bring in those unions.

It was appalling to see men going down, of a frosty morning, with a shovel in their hand and lining up waiting for the boats to come in. The stevedore picked his favourites and if one of the men hadn't a shovel, one of those who had would pass it on so as not to deprive him of that few hours work.

They were paid so little that the unfortunate Missus, when he did get the job, would have to go and borrow one and sixpence or two shillings to release his coat from the pawn. The way things are going it won't take us much longer to get the pawn shops back, although we do have them in the building societies.

That's another thing. The priest used to get up on the pulpit and denounce women, fish women who gave a shilling on loan. You'd buy a shilling's worth of fish and they loaned you a shilling. The priest used to get up on the pulpit and tell them to their faces they were damned because they charged threepence to the shilling.

The Jew who loaned you a pound and charged you twenty five per cent for it, he was damned. Now we have the building societies and insurance companies and what are they when all is said and done but money lenders? There's no one getting up and saying they're damned or they're going to hell. They're charging nine and a half to twenty per cent interest on their loans to young people who are getting married and who have only a couple of hundred pounds to put down.

I can't separate the people who are running building societies from the fishwomen who sold around Parnell Street and George's Street. To me they're money lenders not building societies, they're money lenders and that's what they are. In my time those people were condemned from the pulpit for what they were and what the building societies are today.

When people talk to me about the good old days, I can't see anything good about them. Now, I have the comparison of that time and today and I know that my mother would still use her old phrase, 'Put a beggar on horseback and he'll ride to Hades,' about those in Leinster House.

Jean Roche

We were a very close knit family. My granny ruled the roost. She ruled everything with her nature. She didn't live with us but around the corner in the flats in Benburb Street.

My earliest memories are of looking through my granny's windows on a Saturday night. The street would be littered with papers. I often wondered why it was like this. Another memory was of the horses and carriages, and the drays that carried the barrels of porter from Guinness's.

My granny was in Cumann na mBan from her early days. Her son-in-law always said that was the reason why England left. She was a very positive person and she worked in the Magazine in the Phoenix Park. Before that she had her own horse and cart and she used to go around on her own selling coal. She told me once she carted stones of coal up tenement stairs with her belly under her chin. She didn't think it did her any harm.

Then she went to work in the Mendicity Institution, and I suppose between the Mendicity and the Jameson's Brewery where my grandfather worked, I was rared. It wouldn't happen now, but in a sense it was the equivalent of crèche facilities, you just brought your kids along.

The Mendicity to me was a wonderland out on the quays. There was a very imposing front on the house. The down-and-outs went in along the side and down into the yard. There were colossal kitchens underneath, with big, huge, black iron vats, where they cooked porridge in the morning and stew for the evening meal. There were big black and white tiles on the floor and long wooden benches where the poor people came in. My granny kept it all very regimented and ordered as well as organising the food. No one dared say a word. You got your two slices of bread and your bowl of stew. You sat down with your knife and fork and spoon in order. If anybody messed she just picked them up and threw them out.

I don't think they ever really got knives. Mostly spoons. I remember later when the Institution moved to Island Street their menu became a bit broader, they actually added turnips to the stew. It was very basic at the time.

I remember rambling through the old house in the early mornings, going up and down the wide stairs and going into the Board rooms with the big long tables. A big suit of armour stood in the hall. It was a fantastic place. At one time it was the home of the Earls of Moira and it was here that Pamela, the wife of Lord Edward FitzGerald, was staying when he was arrested in 1798.

My grandad used to take me over to Jameson's with him. I'm not sure what he did, but he must have been some kind of caretaker or maybe he weighed the horses. I used to sit in the office in a large building over in John Street. As a child it always looked big, but even now it looks larger than life, big and imposing. I often pass by just to get the feel of it. I love the feel of it. I used to sit up on the desk and look out the window. The horses and carts came in onto the platform and they would be weighed. My grandad used to bring me into the big rooms, with huge vats and I used to imagine if I fell in I'd never be found, never ever again.

But the men who worked there used to drink an awful lot as well. My granny would be furious at my grandfather if he came home drunk with his bottle of 'first shot'. I also remember my grandfather bringing me down to the pub with him when he was out of work. He would sit me down and buy raspberry for me while he would have his pint. He had a black moustache and he used to say to me, 'I have this moustache because when I take a sup of the pint and lick it I get two drinks.'

After my grandfather died I used to get the pension for my granny and the bottle of whiskey which they used to give to all their pensioners. I did this on a Friday afternoon after school. The men, all my grandfather's age, would be there standing in line with big thick wax moustaches and top hats. Immediately a woman or a child came in they would be put at the top of the queue. Even then I knew I wasn't entitled to just walk in, in front of everyone else, but the men would be offended if you didn't.

When the family was rehoused in Ballyfermot I still went to school in Liffey Street. It was a colossal school to me then. One teacher would teach four classes. Most of the time I would know what was going on in seventh class. I would be learning what they were learning and not my own stuff. I really had completed the six standards of schooling when I left, although I hadn't reached school leaving age.

When my father got sick and my mother was taken into hospital I had to stay home and look after the kids because I was the eldest of nine. I was given permission to stay out because Ballyfermot was so far away. It seemed so far to everybody, even the school inspectors, so it was accepted that I would be out.

When my mother came out of hospital and everything was sorted out I stayed home for a little to mind the kids while she went to work in the convents on a Sunday or a Monday.

The bus conductors knew all the women and they never had a penny. They would let them go on the bus for nothing, they'd come home on the same bus and they'd pay their busfare on the way back. There was this great feeling between people then.

The first job I got was in Grafton Street over Leveretts and Fry's, that's gone now. I hated it. I then got a job in a shop in Thomas Street. I had to stand in the lane out the back with the boss asking me to recite, 'Sixteen ounces one pound, fourteen pounds one stone...' and I had to rhyme all this off before he gave me the job. Then he said to me, 'If I were you now, I wouldn't mix with any of them in there.' He mustn't have trusted them or else he didn't want any rapport between his workers.

I came out of work that Wednesday, thinking I was great with my half day and covered in flour which I'd been weighing all morning. My mother was outside waiting for me and she told me I was going back to the factory. My father insisted also that I go back. They said they couldn't have me running up and down a shop for people. I had to get my trade. In the long run I went back.

I got a job in a sewing factory and I didn't like that either. I got my job in the factory because my father insisted that we have a trade. He felt that as long as you could make something with your hands you'd never be short. It turned out to be true as it happened. Even now I still work at it and I suppose it's the only job you can get now in Dublin. There was a time you could go from one factory to another within an hour and get a job in any of the little upstairs places in the tenements.

My father had a great influence on my life. From the time I was six he'd sit at night and talk politics to me. He told me all about the North of Ireland and de Valera and his speech to Churchill during the war when Churchill wanted to take over the ports. He made me politically aware, although my development as a feminist was delayed. Because of the type of man he was I never knew that there were men in the world who treated their wives as inferior, or beat them up or came in drunk and caused trouble. I thought every man was like my father. I'll always be grateful to him. We always had so little and yet we had so much. I never felt poverty stricken even though I realise now that we must have been. It just never felt like it.

My father was the first patient in Cherry Orchard. He was in Cork Street Fever Hospital with rheumatic fever. He was then shifted up to Cherry Orchard. He became very ill and we would have starved only for my granny. He was a mechanic up in CIE. All he got in sick pay was one pound seven and sixpence to keep nine kids. So my granny, who was still working in the Mendicity, used to take some potatoes, bread and milk and give them to my mother.

My granny used to take me with her to confession every Saturday in Church Street. I'd sit outside. She was a very big woman. Everything about her was big and loud. She would go in and tell the priest how she had stolen the potatoes out of work and everyone in the chapel could hear her. I'd feel mortified. She'd come out feeling great having confessed all her sins. She'd go to communion on Sunday and then she'd do the same thing on Monday. I asked her why did she keep doing it. But she reasoned that as long as she was forgiven it didn't mean she shouldn't do it anymore.

Dublin to me was Queen Street and Benburb Street and the quays. Everyone says now they hate the smell of the Liffey but to me the smell of the Liffey was the smell of the hops coming from Guinness's. It always makes me feel secure and warm and I love it. I love to get the smell even now, although you don't seem to get it as much.

I used to think that Dublin was really dilapidated and falling down and I loved every new building that went up. I didn't care what it looked like as long as it wasn't falling down and was nice and presentable. Now, of course, with the destruction that's going on I wouldn't agree with it at all. I'd rather have a bit of preservation, although I do think that levelling Benburb Street is right. They should have done that fifty years ago. The housing conditions there were really dreadful. My grandmother and grandfather worked in Jameson's after they came back from America during prohibition. They were apparently well off, according to the other people on the street and could have afforded to move out. But I thought afterwards the only thing vulnerable in my granny, the only insecurity she displayed to me, was her inability to move away from Benburb Street.

I found that most of the people who lived there loved it. I did as well, in that it was home. It wasn't poverty because in our flat there wasn't poverty. My granny would never in a million years accept poverty. She was always out at work. But she worked a lot harder than the money she got paid demanded.

Although the people wanted better conditions they didn't want to move out. I suppose the new inner city houses that they're building now are the answer to people's prayers. At that time people were housed out to places like Ballyfermot to which they couldn't relate. Most of them who did go out came back. I mean my mother came back all the time to her mother's. They always came back into the centre because there was this great sense of community.

It sounds like I'm talking about the 'good old days' and they weren't really good. At the same time there must have been something valuable in it. I remember after I was married, my granny was sick and I went back to stay with her for a few nights. We took turns minding her because she wouldn't even move out then. She was seventy six. There were gangs of fellas around the doors. The person who drove me in said, 'Are you not afraid going in there?' But it would never occur to me to be scared going in there. It just wouldn't occur to me.

I would like to see Dublin reconstructed. We need to move away from the Ballyfermots because people did become alienated when they moved out. They missed the old communities where everyone knew everybody else and everything about you. That's gone. Now, if someone knows something about you it's scandal. It's not the same thing.

In Benburb Street there was a whole way of life and a whole attitude to life. None of the young women were allowed to speak to soldiers because the soldiers' barracks were up the road. If you spoke to them you'd have a bad name. There was a pub right across from my granny's and there was a big barrel with a clock at either end. At the side of it there was a big gate where all the fellas out of work used to sit. Nowadays you'd be afraid to walk by them but they all sat down there playing cards and just passing the time. Overhead someone wrote in big letters

IDLERS PARADISE

With the building of these new houses in the city I feel there's the possibility of restoring the community. Another thing I'd love to have restored is the Dublin accent. Now with the surge of yuppyism a whole new accent has emerged. For me there's nothing like a Dublin accent, especially Irish spoken with a Dublin accent. Even if I don't understand it all, I love it. I'd like that for Dublin and of course I'd like to see people in jobs.

I think the Millennium is a farce and the money that's going to be spent could be far more usefully employed. For instance out where I live, there is no remedial teacher in the school. Even if one school got a remedial teacher out of the money for one year, that would be better and far more valuable than all the Bórd Fáilte hype that is going on now.

I also think that it is representing a false idealistic way of life. You don't hear anything on the radio about Robert Emmet or Thomas Street. You won't hear anything about Connolly and Monto, where Dublin women had to go out and sell themselves to the British soldiers. Or how the people were sacked out of Guinness's and given their fares to England to join the British army. Then, when they came back, they were guaranteed a job in the brewery.

There'll be no class awareness in the whole of the Millennium. In that sense it's going to be lacking. If people are making a contribution then that would be a very positive contribution to make. Shove aside all the glitter and the gloss and the 'Dublin can be heaven with coffee at eleven' attitude. Show the Dublin that was there, and to a large extent still exists, but without the security and the community. Show the kind of protection that the community provided, although it was poverty stricken. The poverty is still there. What's missing now is the community and what has taken its place is total alienation. Dublin could turn into a really horrific place to live in if something isn't done about it.

June Levine

With a name like Levine I've always been conscious that people don't think of you as a Dubliner, they think of you as a Jew. And even if generations before you have lived in Dublin, they still don't realise that you are a Dubliner. For that reason I identify enormously with Joyce's Bloom. Do you remember in the pub when a man says to him, 'Where's your country?' or words to that effect, and Bloom says, 'Ireland', and of course this wasn't accepted.

Dublin is as much my home, my native land, as any Dubliner's. I didn't know any other country until I was well grown. So Dublin is my Dublin as much as anyone's. Except in my case there's a quirk because my mother was a Catholic, a MacMahon, whose family goes back as far as Brian Boru and my father was Jewish, whose family went back somewhere to Lithuania. So growing up I felt a sense of never belonging.

If I was with Catholics I was reminded I was Jewish and if I was with Jews I was always reminded that my mother was Catholic. I can remember an awful lot of anxiety in my life when I realised that people were different and belonged to different religions.

My maternal grandmother, Nanny MacMahon, came from Mullingar. She worked in Clery's as a seamstress and when she met Granda MacMahon, he was a hairdresser. He was later employed in the Irish Army in Baldoyle as a barber. They were quite well off. At first, Nanny MacMahon had a little sewing shop in Liffey Street and Granda had a barber shop beside it. My mother was reared there. She had a nervous disposition which my granny said was due to the fact that she was born in 1916. On her way to the Rotunda Hospital shooting broke out. Two British Army soldiers had to pull Granny down underneath a cart for her safety. The MacMahons were a Republican family and were related to Pádraig Pearse. In 1931 Granny and Granda lost their shops in the depression and they then moved to Pembroke Road.

I was born in the Rotunda when my mother was fifteen and my father was seventeen. My mother never worked before that. She was a convent girl. She met my father at the Stephen's Green picture house. It was a very big romance. He lived in Martin Street and was one of eight.

The usual Romeo and Juliet story got out of hand and I was the result. My maternal grandmother and grandfather took them into their flat, a very large flat in Pembroke Road. Until I was about six and a half I had a little pair of blue rosary beads that I used to take to chapel every Sunday. I can see them clearly and I don't know what happened to them. I can see myself holding the railings with one hand and the rosary beads clutched in the other.

All of a sudden everything changed and instead of this sort of paradise where I lived with my nanny, my uncle John, my auntie Rita and my mummy and daddy, I was catapulted out into the real world.

My mother and father moved to Lennox Place, which, to me as a child did not feel as nice as my granny's. It became a place where I grew aware of my parents' problems, of their struggles to be parents, to make a living and have their own home, whereas before I was just part of the family in Pembroke Road. The older I get the more I realise that the extended family is fantastic for the child, even though it is usually difficult for the adults.

So we moved out and it seemed to me from that day on there was a lot of hardship because my parents were so hell bent on being independent. I always remember my maternal grandmother coming over with all kinds of things. She'd arrive with buttered eggs, or a chicken, from the Monument Creamery, with a white powdery breast; or brown bread and butter she'd made.

Food was a very large part of my childhood. It was in the food that I could see the difference between Jews and Catholics. I could see it in the attitudes to food. I remember for years and years I knew they ate differently.

There was, in fact, a period of my life, albeit brief, when I went to the synagogue on Saturday and mass on Sunday. The whole weekend was mucked up as I spent it in confusion.

Grandfather Levine came from Riga in Lithuania. He was conscripted into the Russian Army at the age of twelve but he ran away to escape from a pogrom. He managed to get to Liverpool where he met my grandmother who was a very strong, tough woman. Indeed, my other grandmother was, too, but in a different way. Granny Levine's parents were also from Riga, but she was born in Liverpool. She was a working class woman who worked at sewing on buttons, whereas Nanny MacMahon was genteel working class. She never raised her voice, she was very gentle. She was just different, while Granny Levine, who had eight children was quite capable of letting a roar out of her that would shake you to your boots.

Granda Levine couldn't get work in Liverpool. A man named Windsomers wrote to him from Dublin offering him a job but Granny wouldn't come. After their third child she changed her mind and Granda managed to get a job in Leplar's on the South Circular Road. A strike broke out and he got no strike pay. One hour after the birth of their fourth child, Granny Levine was back at work, sitting up in the bed sewing on buttons.

As I say, the difference was in the food. Nanny MacMahon would bring a nice polite white powdered chicken, Grandmother Levine would buy a nice big fat hen with plenty of yellow fat in it. From that big hen she could make two days' dinners and a pot of soup and leftovers that she could feed you with on a Monday. There wasn't a part of that hen that wasn't used and indeed I often think there was no beast on this earth more honoured than my Grandmother Levine's sabbath hen.

She'd have the feet, she'd have the neck, she'd have all the giblets. From the feet and the giblets she'd make a soup. She'd put the hen into the soup for about an hour and then she'd take it out and stuff it. She would take the skin off the neck. She'd sew the neck up into a sort of sausage and she'd put a special stuffing into it and then roast it. The hen, even though it had been par boiled, would come to the table golden and crisp, as if it had been roasted. Sometimes half of it was stewed with brown potatoes, carrots, gravy all round it, and dumplings made from matzo meal. The other half was saved and roasted.

Always on the sabbath she had what we called chopped liver. This was beef liver which was boiled and grated. The fat which she saved from the hen was rendered down with onion and used with grated onion to make this liver. So when I started going out to fancy places pâté was no surprise to me and it wasn't half as good as chopped liver.

I went to school in Bloomfield Avenue which was then the Jewish National in Dublin. There were a few second generation but most of us would have been third generation. All the teachers in that school were Catholics or if they weren't Catholics they certainly weren't Jewish. At three o'clock in the day they would go home and the Hebrew teachers would come in and teach us religion.

Now all the days I was in that school I never remember any teacher talking about the Christian religion in any way. Even at Christmas or Easter, when we got our holidays, they never referred to it. Their integrity and the way they dealt with that now impresses me.

The one teacher I remember was Dr Teller. He was a special kind of teacher every child should have. The way he taught religion was that he got you so interested in the Old Testament stories you would be pleading with him to tell you one. He would come in with his sandwiches and his tea and his mittens. He could never keep his class in order and he never tried.

Each day he would share his lunch with some child. He had a tremendous feeling for children. If a child had a cold or a sniffle he'd say, 'Come up here you and sit beside the radiator.' To me the Old Testament was the history of the Jewish people. It was the history of Israel. It was never separated from religion as far as I was concerned. It's only in recent years that I realise that not everybody believes that the Old Testament is the history of Israel.

I left school at about fourteen years of age and went on to learn shorthand and typing. At the time it was considered an enormously respectable thing for a girl to do. My father went to work every day on a bicycle. He left in the morning at about 7.45 am and arrived home when it was getting dark.

I think I was about nine or ten when we went to live in Kimmage. The reason for this was, I suspect, that it was safer there than being beside the canal. But I'm not sure why.

Life was a little more difficult for me there because, and I have to say this, on my Jewish side they never made such a fuss about my Catholic side, but the Catholics made an awful fuss about my Jewish side. They would torment me, asking me what I was eating. Of course in the Jewish school they would ask if you ate bacon or did you eat ham, which was a terrible sin. But you got it more on the other side.

Growing up I had two sets of festivals, Passover and Easter, Christmas and Hanukkah, which sounds festive and a great feast, but I always had to keep one

106

set of festivals secret from one part of my friends. So if I was with Jewish friends I couldn't admit that Santa had come to our house because he didn't go to Jewish houses. And if I were with Christian kids I couldn't admit that we celebrated Passover. After all it didn't go down well mentioning Jewish festivals as the Jews had killed Christ.

The result was that growing up in Dublin, after I left my nanny's in Pembroke Road, I was always full of anxiety, of not knowing, of not belonging. So reading Joyce, even though he wasn't recognised, was great in my eyes since he understood what the outcast feels like. The outcast who hasn't done anything. Poor old Bloom! What did he ever do? He didn't do anything but he felt out of it. It's a marvellous portrayal of how people feel when we don't accept them because they're a bit different or they come from a different place.

This is why the women's movement meant so much to me when I was still torn by all that conflict. It was only in the 70s I realised that my people weren't Jews and they weren't Catholics. They were women. This was for me the resolution of that conflict.

Now, the best thing that I ever did for my family was to marry a Jew. I think that if I had come and said to my father I wanted to marry a Christian he would have thrown one of his famous tantrums and probably had a stroke. But as things happened I did marry a Jew.

I always remember that first Christmas we spent together. I bought him a Christmas present and filled his stocking up, he burst into tears that day. I was very surprised. Then he told me that when he was a little boy all the kids on his street were Christians and got great toys and great books. All he ever got was an orange.

When we lived in Kimmage there was no one around to play with except Catholics and I had lots of friends. We used to go to the pictures in the summer. At that time we lived in a little house, and it was attached to a corporation scheme, with a wall running between us and the scheme. There was a watchman put on the wall to make sure that the kids from the corporation houses could not get into the swankier section of private houses.

There was also an older kid put on watch to check that these kids didn't take a short cut through our houses to the shops. The kids out on the street had a song which went:

Oxy Oxy here's the corporation
Oxy was the man on the wall. That's what they used to shout.
Oxy Oxy here's the corporation

Oxy would tear out to kill the kids who were taking the short cut to the shops. Eventually that wall came down. The kids on the other side bored a hole in it and it collapsed. There was this constant battle of tuppence looking down on a penny ha'penny. It was war, and I was one of those kids who was told that they were undesirables, not even that they were undesirables, but that they simply weren't allowed in. We weren't to associate with them.

Then we moved back to Dufferin Avenue. I think my father wanted me to mix with Jewish children now that I was growing older. He was thinking of marriage because most of the Jews were encouraged to marry young, and most do marry young, it's a Mediterranean thing. In Dufferin Avenue all my friends were Jewish. there were no Christian children there.

107

Women used to sell fish all along Clanbrassil Street. On Tuesday and Thursday they sold it in prams and they sold it to Jewish housewives. There was great fun with all the bargaining. The Jews used to live on fish because meat was expensive and kosher meat was more expensive than any. We were eating fish when Christian families were turning it down. From this they used to make gefilte fish. That's three different types of fish, chopped up, filled with crumbs and onions then fried.

I distinctly remember shortages of food in Blarney Park although my father had a plot for vegetables. During the war Daddy made us clogs from wood because the money wasn't there to buy shoes. Also the plot fed us vegetables. It was in Blarney Park off Kimmage Road.

We had the glimmerman and he caused us a lot of heartache, so my father devised this thing: it was a can full of sawdust which he had taken from my grandfather's factory. With the broom handle he dampened the sawdust and made a hole down the middle of it. Then he lit it and it smouldered away and you could boil a kettle on it.

The neighbours would come around and he'd make them one and we'd have them in the back yard, smouldering away so that we could thumb our noses at the glimmerman.

When we came back to Dufferin Avenue there was a much more Jewish atmosphere. Now when I look back the sense of community was much stronger. Everyone knew who you were, who your family was, and you couldn't go into a house on South Circular Road without someone offering you a bite to eat. 'Ah sure you'll have a bite, you'll have a cup of tea.'

I never knew 'till years later that these women came from the ghettos in Europe and it was impossible to tell whether they and their families had enough to eat themselves. Sometimes you'd suspect they didn't. The normal thing to do was to feed a child and not ask questions about home. Any child around was given food. The most common thing to be given was plaice fried in oil, allowed to go cold and then put under a wire safe and served with horseradish and a piece of bread.

The thing that you had to understand about the emphasis put on food in Jewish families was dietary laws in relation to Judaism and that food and comfort were all these people had to give each other. Although Dublin was safe they didn't believe that it was. They had looked at the map and said that's far enough away. Then they came to places like Belfast and Dublin and when they arrived they made a cocoon of the family and food was the currency of a mother's comfort. That was it.

So there was a great emphasis on food, on not eating food that wasn't kosher, as well as on religious matters and on not riding on a bus on the sabbath. You had to walk. It didn't matter how far you had to walk. Certainly if you didn't walk you would be seen not to walk.

I remember Greenville Hall where I was married. That was only around the corner from me, and it was always full. You went there for Yom Kippur or on sabbath. You'd get all dressed up to go to the synagogue. If you were a girl you'd go to the balcony and look down at the men being important.

What I always remember about the synagogue is that everybody talked because the service was very long. It wasn't like a church. The men would talk and clap until the rabbi would get irritated and he would look up at the gallery and

Clodagh Boyd

say, 'Quiet.' He wouldn't disrespect the men by telling them to shut up but he would look up at us and we mightn't be talking at all.

On Yom Kippur we used to fast all day. Yom Kippur is the Day of Atonement. You were supposed to go to the synagogue and confess your sins communally. Then you had to fast in order to atone and so you began all over again.

For us as kids, Yom Kippur was fasting and dressing up and going to all the synagogues in Dublin, you had to walk because you couldn't take a bus. It's in October and yet I remember it as being hot.

We spent the day walking from one to the other. Until that was done, you couldn't have a drop of water. Then we'd come home and break the fast with the whole extended family.

There was a synagogue just around the corner from us, Greenville Hall. That's not a synagogue anymore. There was also one in Lennox Place where I went with my grandfather and uncles when I was little. It was over a shop and it had a Mogen David, a Star of David in coloured glass. It was a proper synagogue, but very small. That's gone also and when I was there recently I noticed that precious piece of glass is gone too. I don't know who took it.

Now there's a museum with a lot of those artefacts in it. It's on Walworth Road. There was the Adelaide synagogue which is still there, it's a fine synagogue; and then there's one in Terenure. I'm sure I'm skipping one. I know there was one on the northside of the Liffey. But those were ones that I knew myself.

There were two secret organisations which looked after poor Jews in Dublin. They were sworn to secrecy because they believed that if anything was said about helping people it would undo the good. One was the Dorcas Organisation for settling poor brides, it would buy all the bride's requirements and pay necessary expenses. My aunt Zelda helped in the other, which visited poor Jews in their homes. One family she visited was in Henrietta Street.

I also remember old people in the community, and everybody doing things for them. The strange thing about the Jewish community is that most of them came from backgrounds of terrible trouble. For instance my ex-mother-in-law was one of two survivors of a family of thirteen who had been killed and raped in Russia. Her two sisters had been raped to death by soldiers. And yet amongst those people there was silence about these things. They never told you. They told you to mind your religion, pray to God and do what the Torah said, 'Follow the way.' But they never bred hate. I never remember being told, they did this to us and they did that to us. Truthfully they never did that, to my knowledge.

I'm talking about the paternal side of my family, but my memories of the other side are tremendously supportive as well. My mother's family in those days, so it seemed to me, was no different. The only difference to me was food as I've said.

The two families never mixed. As I grew older I recognised a certain discord between them. As a child neither said anything about the other to me. I got the same kind of treatment in both houses. The emphasis might have been different, but anything that was to be given in either house I got.

This may have had something to do with my being the first grandchild on both sides. But if only they could have treated each other the way they treated me.

The Jewish community, when I was growing up, was quite large. There were five thousand families, approximately, and a large community in Cork and in

Dublin. But after the state of Israel was declared an awful lot of them went there. You see, a great many Jews dreamt of having a place they'd never be shunted out of. They had gone through the most terrible, terrible strife.

I remember I had a cousin who was brought over here in the late 1930s. Her name was Yetta and she was from Poland. She came to visit my grandfather. She was a bit older than me. On her way back to Poland something happened and she finished up in a concentration camp. Terrible things befell Yetta and she was never heard of again until after the war when she was found in Israel.

The stories of the Jewish people and the fear they had come from made them glad to work at anything, to live on as little as they could, to say their prayers, to help one another, to do anything that would help them to live in peace.

A lot of Jews felt they belonged to Ireland but it took a generation to feel that way. My old school friend Marie Walsman, whose father was the butcher, was from Belgium. I remember Marie's mother. She always had little delicacies for us to eat, but she used to cry every day. Marie told me this. She cried because her family was still left in Europe, and she was here. They lived comfortably. She had a safe home but still she cried everyday. She took her engagement ring off and sold it to send the money to her family. I'll never forget Marie telling me, 'Mammy says how could she wear diamonds on her finger when her family could be starving.' It took time to build up trust.

The Jewish population here has decreased dramatically. Partly because of emigration, after the declaration of the state of Israel, and also because there was very little choice for children who wished to marry. Although the community was large then, the boys you met were more like brothers than boys. Everybody knew everybody else.

There are only a few hundred families left now. There is no Jewish shopping centre. You walk down Clanbrassil Street and all the shops are gone. The places where we used to buy our Jewish food, like the unleavened bread for Pesach, the pickled cucumber, the roll mops, the home baked biscuits, the little coconut pyramids, the almonds that were for special occasions, all those shops have gone. The Rubinsteins have gone. Walsman has retired. The Goldbergs have gone. Where are they? They're all gone. The little draper run by the Zanskys is gone.

When they talk about running a road through Clanbrassil Street, the street they're talking about is gone. That street was a community. When you walked down that street people were trading in the middle of it. People would roar out at you as you passed by and you'd go into the shop and the shopkeeper would say, 'You told me to keep this for you and I have it,' and he'd leave the other people standing.

Long ago the fishwomen stopped coming. Long ago.

Evelyn Owens

I was born in Clontarf and have lived all my life there with the exception of four years. I am essentially a northside Dubliner. I would not maintain that Clontarf was typical of the northside of Dublin, but from the point of view of association with Dublin and being so near the city centre, I feel it is an integral part of the çity. Clontarf was a rather privileged area to grow up in, lying just three miles from the centre of the city. When I was growing up it almost had a community village spirit all of its own. Unless you lived between the Howth Road on the west side and Mount Prospect on the sea road you were not really considered part of Clontarf.

The difference between it and other areas is that it has marvellous natural resources. As kids we did not have to think of what we would do with our leisure time. We had this marvellous expansive sea, the Bull Wall, with all its magic, its sand dunes for playing in and jumping on. We learned to swim by jumping in off the rocks.

When you got a little more sophisticated you could scrounge a few pence off your mother and go off to Clontarf baths. We'd throw each other into the pool in our clothes and the attendant dragged us out, dried us off and told us not to come back for another week.

You had every form of outdoor activity in Clontarf, all available for practically nothing. At one stage we had four tennis clubs which we joined as children, three tennis clubs where Roman Catholics would play and one which was totally Protestant. We were warned at school not to even stop outside to look in at the people playing tennis. I don't know if they thought we would be grabbed and taken into the folds of the dissident church. We did not mix at all with any of the children who attended Protestant schools nor they with us. When we grew up I think most of us had enough wit to get over that sort of nonsense. Way back Clontarf was a Protestant dominated area and so they built their own facilities. You had three Protestant churches as opposed to two Catholic. But now the whole balance has changed.

When you arrived at the teenage stage you did a 'line' with Clontarf people. An amazing number of my friends married locals. There was a high degree of intermarriage. I don't know if that was good for the genes of Clontarf or not. But it had that sort of spirit which I think was unique and one which we can appreciate a lot.

We also had hockey and cricket clubs and a very good dramatic society which only died out in the 1960s when television took over. We also had a musical society.

One of my most abiding memories as a youngster in Vernon Gardens was running in to get a jam jar from my mother to swap for a balloon from the balloon man. I don't know when the balloon man disappeared. He was probably killed in the war.

I started school in the Holy Faith Convent in Clontarf. During the war, or the 'Emergency' as we knew it, I remember the vast Corpus Christi procession. It used to start in St John the Baptist Church. As you progressed you got yourself into a choir so that you could stay in the organ loft throughout the procession, otherwise you queued up for half an hour to join whatever grade or sodality you were in at school.

In the procession there was a mixture of the Belgrove Primary School, the Holy Faith, Clontarf and organisations which came during the Emergency, the Local Defence Force, the Local Security Force, and the Red Cross, the Sea Scouts, the Boy Scouts and the Girl Guides. They all had their banners and the procession took off around three on Sunday afternoon and wound its way up Vernon Avenue and into the grounds of Belgrove School where you had outdoor benediction. We had bands and a choir and they were broadcast from St John's. It then wound its way down and into the church for another benediction. It broke up around six o'clock. It was really very spectacular and impressive and I suppose a great outpouring of religious devotion as well. I think it would have been a unique person who did not participate in the procession at the time.

I can't remember a family holiday and I don't think that very many people had holidays in that era. Money was not available during the war years. We did get the occasional trip to the country to stay with the relations for a fortnight, once every three or four years. I never missed not going away on holidays because we had so much going in Clontarf that it really did not matter.

Summer seemed to be totally blissful. I spent my time going to the tennis clubs in the morning and down the Bull Wall or for a swim in the evening or the other way around if the tide was right. We all had bicycles which we went out on in the evening and chased one another around the place.

At the stage when we were interested in boys or boys were interested in us we would meet at the crossroads in Vernon Avenue or at the top of Belgrove Road on the way home from school. We had a local curate who was very anti the idea of boys and girls talking. So the big trick was not to get caught by Fr O'Keeffe on his bicycle coming home in the evening. If you did you just jumped over a garden wall and hid. That was our introduction to company keeping.

I left school and started work in Dublin Corporation. I might have had other ideas of what I wanted to do but it was not possible in the family circumstances. I was glad to have a job and earning a few bob. The depressing thing, when I think back on that period, was the cycle to and from work, four times a day as I came home for lunch. I came in through Summerhill and the absolutely awful sight always stuck in my mind. This was before they did the reconstruction job in the

50s, which I never agreed with. In that period youngsters went to school in their bare feet and torn jumpers with their elbows out and patches all over the place. They were terribly poor. It was my first insight into poverty. I witnessed it every time I went to work. Nowadays there is a striking difference between the old and the new housing. We all know there is poverty and it is getting worse but relative to the period in 1948 things are very much better.

The other big change I see is the size to which Dublin has grown, but the expansion of the city has not been good for Dubliners. People in the country complain that there is too much centralisation. Dubliners agree, because it spoils their city. To go to Bray or the mountains now takes so long you just don't bother. In extending Dublin we have lost the caring neighbourhood we had and I find that distressing.

I loved Saturday night in O'Connell Street. You went in to meet your friends, or your date, at the Metropole, beside a telephone box or under Clery's clock. Then you went to the Savoy or to Cafolla's for an ice cream. It was teeming with life. You had people going into the dress dances in the Aberdeen Hall and sure if you'd nothing else to do you could always sit in the Gresham and watch them go in and see who was dating who. I've seen O'Connell Street very early in the morning without all the traffic and it's beautiful. Now it just depresses me because at eleven o'clock at night you don't even have the queues of people for the last bus, like you used to. O'Connell Street has no life left in it. That is one of the most striking and sad changes that I see and I think it's brought about by sheer fear. I'm not a nervous person by nature but I find myself walking around my own city constantly having to mind my handbag or wondering whether I will bring one at all. It was fun window shopping, even if you never spent a penny or never went back to buy one of the outfits.

The increase in the number of cars has altered city life. In the olden days there were thousands of bicycles. It's good to see them coming back, although it's a nightmare when you're driving.

The other awful thing is the dreadful pollution. I walk a fair bit now and to see and feel the smog is terrible. We used to joke with English visitors years ago about their smog saying, 'When the smog lifts you can see the rain.' It's true of Dublin now and it's quite frightening. I would not go for a swim now in the Bull Wall. I grew up there, I went with the tide there, I used to swim in the morning before going to work. I got into it about two or three years ago and said, 'Never again.' That fact is denying a lot of Dublin people a free outdoor activity. Swimming pools are grand for teaching kids and it's great to have them, but they're not nearly as nice as the sea.

My first priority for change would have to be jobs. Until we can come to grips with and defeat the unemployment problem I don't think Dublin is going to be a happy city in the true sense. I don't think we can be justifiably happy when we see so much misery around us, when there is so much deprivation and emigration.

There have been several efforts made to draw up a plan for local government organisation but most of it has to do with specific ideas about what should be done in the Dublin area and for whatever reason none of them have ever been followed through. No government has had the political strength or will to implement them. We are now still operating, more or less, with structures that were set up in 1898 and have only been tinkered with ever since. Until we get that right we're only groping towards the Dublin I want to see. I would like to see

Lucy Johnston

more women at the top of the administration in local government because they can bring a particular angle or slant into local government issues.

Music suffered with the loss of all the old music halls and the orchestra having to be more or less mobile. The National Concert Hall is a great achievement, it has brought a lot of cultural activity and the spin off is the revival of interest in music in the city, even if it has been more localised around the pubs, particularly jazz. That's been great because music is still cheap here and you can listen to good music in Dublin. There is a bit of revival in the theatre, though not as much as music.

I hope the millennium will bring about a revitalisation of the city. I would like to see Dublin people really caring for their city again. I think it's going to be good fun for Dubliners and I hope we'll have a lot of activities we don't usually have. I hope we'll get more tourists who will bring in a bit of money into the city.

Marjorie Hampton

I come from a middle class background. We lived on a road in Ranelagh where there were not many Church of Ireland families, perhaps four houses out of seventy or eighty, the rest were mostly Roman Catholics.

What I remember most about those early years is that, in some respects, we were different. Being Protestant, we were very defensive. We were looked on as having an Anglo Irish background. Therefore, we felt we were a race apart. The people were very neighbourly but they didn't really make friends with us.

On Sundays we went to church and then to Sunday school. We came home and we went back out to children's service in the afternoon. We were different, there was no doubt about it. The Catholic children went to mass in the morning and played football or went to the pictures in the afternoon. We looked on that as completely wrong.

We never complained about being on the defensive. It was only when we were growing up in the early to middle 50s, we decided to stand up and speak. We began to talk about being a part of Ireland, being part of Dublin. It was what we wanted. We weren't staying in our little circles any longer.

This is when I became aware that I was Irish born and bred and that I had nothing to do with any other country. I wanted my Ireland. From the 50s on, things definitely changed. You were able to speak out and you were a person in your own right. You were no longer set apart as a Protestant. There was a definite easing.

Life was still very difficult in the parish because we had Roman Catholic friends whom my family accepted, but if you brought them to another house they might not be accepted. It was a most peculiar thing. I can't really understand how we let ourselves get so narrow.

A Roman Catholic couldn't really marry a Protestant but a Protestant could marry a Roman Catholic, we were losing people from our church and we were no longer going to sit and say, 'Right, there goes another one.'

We decided, as a community, and as Protestants, to hold onto our rights and our heritage. We had something to say and to contribute to the community as a whole. Protestantism is as good as Catholicism, and Catholicism is as good as Protestantism and we wanted to find a happy medium which would allow us to live in tolerance of each other.

Throughout the 50s things improved greatly. The standard of living went up and the job situation got better. It was into the 60s before the banks, Guinness's and Jacob's, opened their doors to other people, before that they had nurtured employees from the Church of Ireland. Unfairly the wealth of those firms was held mostly by Protestant people although the majority of the population was Roman Catholic. As we became more tolerant of each other that changed and people began to get jobs on a fairer footing..

I didn't grow up in dreadful poverty. I didn't even see shocking poverty. The Protestants felt that they were giving the Roman Catholics something. It's funny how this comes over so strongly to me but it does.

Recently I had occasion to leave my son Garret to the boat and I was utterly shocked at what I saw. I was so upset at the poverty that I saw on that boat. I hadn't seen poverty like it since the late 40s to early 50s. Those kids going out on the boat to England brought back, so strongly, how poor we used to be. They had white faces, light clothes and they were thin and weedy. When my son rang me that night I said, 'I'm so shocked at what I saw this morning. The poverty. I really haven't got over it.' He said, 'It's funny, Mum, that you should say that. It was like going on a last journey, with people who have one last hope to do something.'

What distresses me most in Dublin today is the poverty that we're facing again. It's all very well for me. I'm not poverty-stricken. My day is fine. I can do what I want, go where I want, eat if I want and do I ever feel guilty about it? I have these fine high standards of living and ours is a good standard. But does it do me any good? I would love to go out and help people. But the trouble is, what can I do? People are very wary about accepting charity and you can become patronising. What I would like to see is jobs for our young people. We are sending away the best brains because the best brains are the ones who are going to get the best jobs. We're also sending away kids who haven't any qualifications and who have no money in their pockets. This has to be wrong.

There is definitely need for some form of employment, but I'm not happy with these teamwork schemes, or social employment schemes. They are fine for six months but it must be very upsetting for a kid to only get a job for just six months, and there are many firms who give work knowing that there are no 'real' jobs at the end of these schemes.

I don't think the dual carriageway, which will bring traffic into the centre of the city, should be built. It's going to split the community. The argument given out, at times, by the corporation, is that it will bring people back into the city to shop. If you want to go into town to shop, you'll go in if you have a good bus service on the periphery of the inner city area. What Dublin lacks is a good underground system and no one will persuade me otherwise. I think they say we haven't the population for an underground system, but it's a quick way of getting from A to B. Why can't they run this carriageway around the ring of the city or the suburbs and make the fast roads with flyovers? I honestly feel that is the answer. They should leave the inner city as a community centre with a life at night.

If people came back in to live in the centre we would not have the same crime problem. Everything would improve if we had people around all the time. Crime has evolved because people have moved out and the streets are empty.

JAKLEN
LeverArch
FILE

I know the corporation are trying to do things and it's nice to see Grafton Street being pedestrianised. There are so many little streets around that could be pedestrianised fully with no traffic going down them.

It's the eyesores that catch your attention. The sites which have been let slip into a state of dereliction. I don't know what kind of rules the goverment can bring in to say that if people buy a site, like they did in Earlsfort Terrace, it cannot lie idle for ten years before something is done. Obviously there's money to be made in this and someone is sitting back making a fortune out of our city.

I grew up in Rathmines and I love it. My father's name is on the war list there because he fought in the First World War. So did his two brothers. My sister's name is there because she was in the Second World War. I don't want to see that church go. But neither do I see the sense in paying out thousands of pounds in keeping it open for seventy five people.

I know that our Protestant churches have had to close because our numbers are going down. Here I feel my opinion would be at variance with some of my own people, but I believe that some of the churches should be shut. We could get a larger congregation into one particular area for services. What is the use in spending thousands of pounds on the upkeep of St Catherine's and St Kevin's when there's not enough congregation to keep the churches open, particularly in Rathmines and Harold's Cross and Crumlin? I think possibly there's going to be some amalgamation there. I've recently changed my parish. Now that my boys are grown up and have left home I come into the Cathedral. I like the Cathedral and its anonymous air and I love the music.

Harold's Cross and Rathmines are flat dwelling areas with a moving population. If they want to go to church they'll find one. You can't force people into church just because the church is there. It just doesn't work.

If a church has to close it should be used for something else. We closed St Paul's last September and I would definitely approve of what they've done there, they've opened up a community enterprise centre. They put many units into it and created employment in the area. One centre opened in the old Classic cinema in Terenure, where there is a coffee shop, a hair dresser, a craft shop, a shoe repair service and a photographer. I'm sure my own people would shout at me, but a beautiful building like Rathmines Church in the middle of the road could be used as a magnificent community centre and could give employment in the area.

I'm not necessarily saying it should be desecrated. If you look at the Methodist Church in Charleston Road, they've done a beautiful job on the windows and on the whole building. They've done it on the Parochial Hall in Harold's Cross and again they've made a magnificent building out of it.

If we have to close our churches let's make them into something useful. That's what I'd like to see.

Eileen Reid

What nicer front garden could you have than Patrick's Park or what better playground than the Bayno? Well, I had both because I was born in the Iveagh Buildings in Patrick's Street. It was a great place and I loved it. My ma and da are still living there, in D Block right up at the top and all the people I know are still there, too.

My mother and father also went to the Bayno when they were young. Of course, the Bayno wasn't the real name, it was the Iveagh Playcentre, but leave it to us in Patrick's Street to call it the Bayno. It's only now when I look back that I realise that it was a kindergarten. I loved it and it was so well run. The rooms were magnificent and it had lovely maple floors. In the big, big, room upstairs, the women, all dressed in white gear, gave out the buns and cocoa from these huge wicker baskets and large enamel jugs. It was like something you'd see out of *Oliver*. I thought it was fantastic.

It was supposed to be for the poor, particularly for those living around the Iveagh Buildings. They really couldn't let everyone in, only so many, or it would have been over-run. I remember the big yard out the back of the Bayno where we used to play in the summertime, dancing around the Maypole and doing all the sports. At Christmas time we all got lovely presents and I used to be in the pantos and all the other shows they put on. They used get beautiful gear and dress us up. There were also sewing classes and cookery classes and you didn't have to bring a thing, they supplied it all. I was in the cookery class downstairs and it was great. You wouldn't get that today, not for nothing. I loved that time. We didn't miss out in any way and everything was right at hand, the cinema, the shops, the parks.

Just around the corner we had the Iveagh Baths. I used to swim there all the time. The galas were held every Friday night and when I was young I used to wish that I was part of that. I remember Otter and Pembroke swimming clubs, they were ever so snob. I would pay in to have a look at them because I wanted to be part of that scene. Eventually I joined and I started to swim for Guinness's.

I won many prizes and loved it so much that they asked me to swim for Ireland, for their lifesaving. Only four of us were picked and I was only fourteen at the time.

I was never outside of Dublin until my da drove us down to Powerscourt. We always went to Portmarnock during the summer holidays and I think I knew every little grain of sand in it. My ma would bring us out there two or three times a week. I always loved going over the hump backed bridge in the bus which used to pass by the Old Shieling. The houses around there looked like castles to us and we thought that the people who owned them must be loaded. Going along the road I used to say, 'I'm goin' to live in a big house like that when I grow up.' That was my ambition.

Kennedy's Bakery was only across the road and my ma would send me for a loaf or a turnover. That was my favourite, but by the time I'd get to the top of the stairs I'd have a hole dug through it. They didn't have the sliced pan then. When we were hungry we didn't run up the stairs but we'd shout up at the window, 'Ma, Ma, I'm hungry. I want a cut of bread.' She'd do up the bread and the jam, put it in a paper bag and throw it out through the window.

I was only a child in the fifties. I went to school in the Holy Faith in Clarendon Street and left when I was fourteen because it was the done thing then. Would you believe it but my school was where the Westbury Hotel is now! The mammy said, 'You'll leave school now and go into a factory.' That's the only thing I missed out on because if you want to get on in the world you need an education. I was a bit fortunate in a way, in that God gave me a talent, so I was able to do something.

But when I left school I went into a clothes factory in Hill Street. It was called Orr Wear and we made overalls. I was there for a year until I was sacked for laughing. I was sacked for laughing, would you believe it? I was always giggling. Then I went into Jacob's and stayed there for another year. I was on the stock department and I used to shove all the orders across the bridge to the trucks. But that's gone as well. Everything is going. They're doing away with all my background.

In Jacob's on a Friday night all the workers would buy the broken biscuits, a bag for one shilling and threepence. Well, it was one and three if you got the Club Milk. They came in a box but the broken biscuits you got in the strong brown sugar bags. When I think of it, it was great.

It was on a football team for Jacob's that I got the lucky break into show-business. My da used to play football, although he didn't work for Jacob's. I think he played for Guinness's but I'm not sure. He was a footballer and was actually capped for Ireland.

When I got the chance I went into a band, just a small group. From the time I could walk my mother said that I was humming and singing. I was at it all the time. Running up and down the five storeys, I'd be singing away and getting a great echo. I used to go to the dances in the Flanagans,' Nora and Mary and Billy Boyd from the North Strand also used to be there. They asked us to dance in the Royal when we were only twelve but my father wouldn't allow me to. He didn't like the idea of show business. Billy now, he went on the Royal and then went to England. I got an offer to go to London to dance and I couldn't take that either. I faced obstacles all the time. My father wanted me to stick to the swimming because he thought it was a nicer thing to be at. But it was just that I was meant to sing and that was that.

I wanted to do more than just stay around the street so I used to look all around

Stephen's Green, all around town to see if there was a dancing class I could go to. Eventually I got singing in St Francis Xavier's Hall and in Archbishop Byrne Hall. I remember dancing for the Lord Mayor once and I came second in the Queen of Taps, over in Parnell Square. I got a medal and they kept consoling me by saying, 'You'll win next year, you'll win next year.' I used to dance in the Myra Hall in Francis Street too, when I was in the Girl Guides.

We went a lot to the Olympia because it was only around the corner from us but we did go occasionally to the Gaiety. We always went to see the pantos and they are something that I don't think kids should be deprived of. They are just magic and all children should experience that. I think it is disgraceful the way our theatres are run. Both the Olympia and the Gaiety should be open twenty four hours a day. Plays should be on the school curriculum and schools should be going to them. Do you realise that there are thousands of kids who may never realise that the theatre is for them? You see, when adults get older, they get very selfish. You forget the kind of things that made you happy. What could be more exciting than sitting up in the Gods of the Olympia, the band starting and the curtain going up. I always wanted to be a part of that. I wanted to live there in that panto in fantasy land.

The women, when I was young, were fantastic. They were wonderful, ten out of ten to them. I could never be the woman my mother was. When I think of her then, no washing machine in the flat and seven children. I tell you I wouldn't do it. My mother used to scrub clothes in the big steel basin with the big rack. They used to use them in skiffle groups. Her knuckles are still huge from that scrubbing and it had to be done every day. Then she'd have to put the clothes through the old fashioned wringer, that we called, the mangle. We loved doing that for her.

A lot of women went to the Iveagh Market in Francis Street. My mother still goes there to buy her food because it's cheaper. They had a laundry there as well as the food and second hand clothes and I remember seeing the women slaving away in the steam. They had to pull these big presses with all the bars which were real hot and hang all the wet clothes over them while the steam came out roaring. Then they had to push them back into the walls and back out again before they were ready for ironing. Some women from our flats worked there.

The glass houses they are building now in Dublin are terrible and when I think about the dual carriageway it seems like they are going to kill the whole city stone dead. They want to widen the road so that you can go right up to Harold's Cross. The far side of Patrick's Street from us is going to be flattened, but imagine if they start putting up office blocks. The balance would be all wrong.

For tourists to come and look down that road it would be like the bit in the Wizard of Oz, follow the yellow brick road. Why don't they fill in all the potholes and build flyovers? Let them keep away from the centre of Dublin because it's the only thing we have.

I'm delighted with what they are doing with Grafton Street, it looks lovely. A lot of the streets around that area should be pedestrianised, especially around Stephen's Green. There shouldn't be any traffic going round it at all. I can just picture Patrick's Street with lovely cafes to sit out at and trees lining the middle of the road. It could be made like a huge wide avenue. I can hear people say, 'What are they going to do with the traffic?' Well that's their problem. There should be ring roads around the city and no traffic in the centre.

124

Christ Church is lovely, I mean it's in the right place. They shouldn't interfere with anything like that, nor with any of the other churches, like Francis Street, which is beautiful. They're not really featuring these places on the outside. I also think that the likes of places such as Thomas Street should be done up and made into a proper market the same as Moore Street where the dealers could have their stalls done up with character. You know the lovely ones with the big barrels.

It can be done. Look at the improvement in Golden Lane. That was in an awful state, a real eyesore, but now it's fantastic, it's beautiful, looking right out onto Patrick's Park.

Lucy Charles Fitzsimmons

I'm a townie. I was born opposite what was High School in the heart of Dublin. You wouldn't recognise Harcourt Street now with all the buildings. A playground used to be there. Besides that was a Swedish lady who gave dancing lessons and a Swedish gymnasium that became Heiney Petrie's Studio.

I remember going there as a child. It was a big gymnasium with rope ladders which were meant to be good for you. There was also the Harcourt Street laundry in those days. I remember going in there and doing the frills on the pillow slips on the machine. In those days they were very nice, they didn't mind children going around.

There was a paper shop at the end of Harcourt Street that was run by a Mrs Donaghy. She was about four foot high and the counter was up above her head. She'd pop up and down settling the papers.

My father was a doctor and surgeon and he started the skin cancer hospital in Hume Street.

There used to be a lovely little shop that sold things like peggy's leg and lucky packets. The window was plastered with everything. That was just in the corner, I remember it well, as you turn into Camden Street. The shops would send you presents at Christmas, spiced beef and a box of biscuits. Can you imagine them doing it now? Your food used to be delivered in those days free, your potatoes and your meat.

Another place you went to was the Municipal Gallery in Harcourt Street. I spent my childhood running up and down those stairs. I think it's ARKS now, one of those very big old houses.

I don't remember much more about Harcourt Street except that there was a hotel beside us and, of course, the station. Then I went for a while to Alexandra Junior School which was down in the Terrace. I'll never forget going to school. There was a Dr Barron, I don't remember her first name but she was an enormous lady. Head of the children's junior part. She'd frighten the life out of you.

Another thing I remember about Harcourt Street was a big wall around the garden of Iveagh House. It backed on to the laneway behind the row of houses on Harcourt Street. The real thing was, along with my brothers, to get up the telegraph pole and into the forbidden garden. It was a lovely garden. It was like going into another land, full of trees and shrubs.

There was a toy shop called Lawrence's. You were taken there to see the toys, just to see them, that's all. That was in O'Connell Street, I think it was near Nelson's Pillar. There was also Noblet's and that was a great attraction, to see them winding the sugar and elasticised mixture round and round different wheels in the window. It would be made into toffee, there on the spot. That was on Stephen's Green.

Then of course there was Bewley's at the top of Grafton Street. It was most attractive. It had all the oriental nooks and crannies, velvet cushions and backs to the seats so you were in a little enclave by yourself. It was a very exciting place.

I remember 1916 with the shooting in Harcourt Street. I saw a woman shot down in the street. She had a big sack of flour and was covered in blood.

After school I went to the Metropolitan School of Art, which was in Kildare Street, expressly against my father's wishes, a medical family should stick to the steady path. However, what is interesting is that in those days the fees were actually very low and there was no question of refusing anyone on entry. You came in and you paid your money in the Registrar's office. You gave your name and address and your father's job and you paid whatever was to be paid and that was that. The fees were seven pounds for the entire year. People could also have two nights a week for a few shillings, maybe less. No portfolio, nothing like that was needed, just your five and sixpence or whatever it was. Then you gradually found your feet. Nobody told you anything of course. You just found out that there was a series of departmental exams you could take which would qualify you to teach, to paint or become a sculptor.

A silversmith or a goldsmith kept you banging at a pot for a year. If you could suffer that you could go on and do things, but if you couldn't then you gave up. It was a good way of making you see if you were serious or not, hammering out a metal shape.

The sculptor then was Oliver Sheppard who you would remember by the statue of Cuchulainn in the General Post Office. He was a very stout little man, very fat like Mr Domo, very nice.

Gabrielle O'Riordan was in my year. She designed our coins, not Metcalfe's with the horses and the fish, but the Irish interlacing ones. She's dead since. A little before me, there was Frances Kelly, Eavan Boland's mother, who married Freddie Boland, the Irish Ambassador to the United Nations.

The great thing was that the college was run by the Department of Education, and the examinations were based on what had been the South Kensington system. There was also a scholarship. It wasn't very much but it was a very, very prized thing to get because it lasted three years and it only came up every three years and only three were given. There was a prize distribution of one pound. If you won a scholarship you thought you were made.

There was only the Taylor's Art Competition in my young days as a student. You had to win that to get your feet on the ladder. It was big money. £50!

Then, there was this man named Daniel Egan, I think he was the first man to have a night club in Dublin. Of course we didn't go to night clubs but he had a framing place in Merrion Row, a shop with pictures and frames, and he was a great little man for giving students credit. So when you got your prize you went around to get a frame and buy canvas.

Life goes on and I wanted to go away. The thing to do then was to go to France, and it was to Mainie Jellet and Evie Hone you went to for advice and they said, 'Go to Paris of course.' I went to Paris with the help of one of my father's relations. He himself was dead by then and since my education didn't cost a penny, in the sense the fees were so low, I went to Paris to Beaux Arts and then to André Lote which they recommended was the place to go to. He was a very clever man, and a very nice painter too. We were very much influenced by him. He made a lot of money out of foreign students. I don't suppose the fees were a terrible lot but it seemed so then. Four pounds. I was away a long time.

I soon found that this wasn't the way to live. There was no money. So I went to Paul Colan who was a commercial designer and who had a very good studio, very good, I thought. Then I got some freelance textile design in Paris, silk screen, printed design and that earned me a living to a certain extent. Then the second World War broke out and we went home.

When I came back Dublin had gone through a lot of changes. I was offered a small job in the college. I was delighted to get it but it was freezing cold, there was no heating. The only thing to heat anywhere was wet turf. Some people used to take home a sod of wet turf in their attaché cases and put it in the gas oven, to dry it. If a knock came to the door you'd be afraid to open it in case it might be the glimmer man.

I lived in Baggot Street, which was always a nice street because you had the trees down the centre, it was always attractive. But there was a lot of austerity with the blackout during the war. There wasn't as much social life then as there is now. Although we'd plenty of food there was a shortage of heating. We had no hot water and you went home with your friends for a bath if they had hot water.

If you were established you were employed by the Department of Education, you were a civil servant. But most of the teachers were part-time. They wouldn't be pensioned off and there'd be no security of tenure. You could be let go tomorrow.

We had a Dutch man as a professor of design and I went on to become his assistant. I did take a job for the Department of Education, as Inspector of Schools. A wonderful way to get to know the country. You went to Sligo one week, and then you went down to Kinsale or Cork. The trains were out of this world. They were cutting the wood down as they went along to keep them going. So you got used to sitting, like a commercial traveller, in a train that sat in one place for a couple of hours. I eventually got Professor Romein's position when he retired, and life went on.

English people would come over by the Claude and have steaks. Though I don't know if we were that wealthy having steaks. The Red Bank Restaurant and the Dolphin were the place to go. The Dolphin had an open charcoal grill, you chose the steak and they put them on the grill, on a big range in the Dining Room.

There are some things I like to know I started. One, which has gone on to very great heights, is in the fashion world. I started the connection with Telefis Eireann. We had a lot of openings for a lot of people in that work. We had a series of lectures by various designers. Alpho O'Reilly, the Mitchells, who I think have gone since, they were from Canada, and a woman who has just retired from RTE

128

named Lona Moran. Patricia Murray was an early student in the college and she was one of the first on the Committee for Fashion. I think she's just retired from the college board now.

The College, when it left Kildare Street, moved around for a while, the quays, Clarendon Street and various factories, before finally settling in Thomas Street. There was a lot of discussion at the time about the suitability of Thomas Street. In fact I would have said Belfield was a better place because you'd be mixing with architects and designers in engineering. Graphic design is one thing but product design is another. There you'd have had an interchange of disciplines which could have been very beneficial.

I exhibited at the Academy. I was a realist painter not an abstract painter. It was terribly hard to sell. Waddington was the man who came to Dublin to put art on the map. And he did a lot of good. You couldn't compare the situation now with then. I think that the print jobs that have come on the scene in Dublin have popularised paintings.

Dublin has changed, attitudes have changed. The language people use now you didn't hear when I was a child, much less discuss what is the norm nowadays.

People were more concerned with the appearance of the city then, there was more discipline. You didn't throw your rubbish out on the street. Perhaps you didn't have so many paper packages to get rid of. Now with our affluent society there is so much packaging and decorations. And what do we do with these things? There is such a lot of rubbish to be got rid of.

When I was young my home wasn't concerned with things like the arts, or the environment. It was more you were brought up where God put you and you stayed there. You couldn't get out of it.

Catherine Donnelly

I was born in Dublin and went to school in Mount Anville from when I was five. My family lived in Carlow but in 1961 we moved to Dublin, to Monkstown. Part of my memories of Dublin are of a very glittering city. You came up for shopping and then you went back to school which wasn't very pleasant. The shopping trips were full of excitement. Lunch in the Hibernian Hotel. You'd come home laden with parcels.

In those days there was a great difference between country and city. Things weren't accessible. Nowadays you can go into any little town and find things you want. But then it seemed to be a treasure trove.

Dublin had the same sort of atmosphere that New York would have for me now. The same sort of buzz. It felt a little bit different at school, in that we thought Dublin was sophisticated and seemed to be in the hub while we were locked up in the country.

When we moved up, although I'd been to school in Dublin, I think I was quite lonely, solitary, I'd been used to my own company. Even though I was quite gregarious I explored Dublin by myself. I remember the seaside. We'd swim down in Seapoint and it was lovely. I thought it was fantastic that you could walk down from a house in the city and swim in this very clean water.

In those days it was a friendly place. You never felt threatened or frightened nor did your parents worry when you disappeared for eight hours. They might be moderately angry when you came home but you weren't lying in a ditch unless you'd been run over by a car. It was very friendly and manageable. Dublin had a very elegant quality to it then with all the hotels. The Russell and the Hibernian and briefly, Jammet's, which closed down quite quickly when I was about eighteen. That would have been around 1966.

Dublin had a lovely elegance about it and everyone seemed to be sucked into it, no matter what their income. We went into the Hibernian lounge when we were college students and had fifty pence and no one threw you out unless you were drunk and disorderly. All those were very gentle, elegant aspects of Dublin which seemed to be accessible to everyone.

I just missed the end of the literary side of Dublin. I was too young to appreciate that I should have been looking at Dublin people who were very interesting. I didn't meet them but I do remember seeing Paddy Kavanagh and others like him, in The Bailey Pub. Just talking about The Bailey reminds me that it was owned by John Ryan. He was a great literary figure. His mother owned the Monument Creamery.

There weren't any supermarkets and there was a great thing about going to different shops for different things. My mother used to make life difficult for herself this way. We used to buy butter in the Monument Creamery and they used to slap it with great wooden paddles, then bacon in Findlater's and sausages in Byrne's of Chatham Street. There was a shop at the top of Stephen's Green, Smith's of the Green, I can't remember what we got there but this would have been the circuit we followed on our trips.

The Bailey was an incredible place. It hadn't been refurbished then as it is now. It was, later, by John Ryan, but at that stage it was all nooks and crannies and there was an old barman there who was great. He was a friend to everyone. I remember all the different rooms and the seafood bar with oysters and fresh prawns on the left. It's just so sad that there's nothing like it left in Dublin. You couldn't have found anything as good as it in the world. It was just so perfect. Then later it had to be done up. I'm sure it had to be falling down with all the different stairs going up to different rooms and bars.

The same could be said of Jammet's, even with mice running all over the place. I remember going there as a guest with a man, and the waiters were so nice. I was an incredibly gauche seventeen year old. Christine Keeler was having lunch there and my mouth was hanging open for the entire repast. It was well after the scandal and I remember thinking that she should have been more glamorous. She looked kind of tired and grimy.

During my schooldays, I remember going into the cinema for three and sixpence. You'd go into the Metropole and they'd turn a blind eye to the fact that you were fifteen and drinking Carlsberg Specials and you were moderately drunk after two of them.

I used to travel home to Monkstown on the 46A bus which would take an hour and a quarter all along a winding little road, through Stillorgan. I must have been barely seventeen because I had been in Mount Anville for eleven years which was quite sufficient.

Having spent all that time in a convent school, I initially chose Arts in college. Eventually I read law in UCD which had the advantage of being 98% male and not a nun in sight. It was around the swansong of Earlsfort Terrace. We all thought it was dreadful, because we thought Trinity was wonderful. But once we all got into it, it was good.

My first year was fairly miserable, being thrown into university from a boarding school was difficult. I think I was a little sudden for the people there as well. I used to wear black nail varnish with white targets on it and a lot of boys in the class thought this a little sudden.

The college moved out to Belfield after I left. I failed exams there for many years. I kept doing the BCL and failed and failed and failed and failed and kept repeating. When I could no longer repeat I went direct to the BL which you could do. Finally I got the BCL.

College life seemed very small, everyone knew everyone else. There were people who shone there. I didn't have a very high profile when I was at university, but some people did and they are still around, some of them. Others seemed to just peak at that time.

There was a little aspect of student life which necessitated staying up for twenty four hours a day for weeks before the exams. There wasn't a great deal of time spent on work in the interim. That was when some people's entrepreneurial skills surfaced.

A guy started a dress hire business, charging just a tiny bit less than the other dress hire outfits. It was so obvious and so clever, because of those wretched dances you have to go to when you are in college. They cleaned up.

The relationship with Trinity students was normal. We had friends in Trinity and we'd go down for lunch to the Buttery. The Trinity students hadn't a hope in hell of getting a bite to eat. We'd all be sitting there in the Main Hall or in the Buttery eating our plates of stodge. Then they introduced cards. People had friends, but there wasn't a real contact. We drank in different pubs, for convenience sake. One year O'Dwyer's would be the place to be in and the next it would be Hartigan's. Trinity had a bar of its own plus the ones down around there. I had a couple of friends in Trinity but I don't know how we got to meet one another, at parties, I suppose.

Then I got into King's Inns and I followed the same pattern as the earlier exams, just getting them at the second half. Today I think it's still the same, this archaic way of life which seemed very irrelevant to society, it's like the late nineteen hundreds.

You had to have four King's Inns' dinners per term or you couldn't do your exams. The great trick was to slip in late. You had to wear black dresses, but I used to wear black trousers which was close enough. You went into the lodge and each diner was signed in, that way they knew if you had attended or not. At the end of the year you might have only done eight dinners instead of sixteen, depending on what numbers you had to do. At the end of your time you had to have done thirty-six dinners in all.

The point of it was you were supposed to sit at tables with people who were more experienced than you, discussing fine points of law and their experiences of them. It was an excellent way of giving a tutorial back in those days. Everyone sat with a qualified barrister at each table. It was a tutorial while you dined and it was quite a social plus. It was a way of selecting friendships, because it thrives on people knowing each other.

I think it still goes on. We'd go in and drink inordinate quantities of beer through the night from big copper urns. Then you could have either a bottle of wine or half a bottle of port on Grand Nights. There was one Grand Night a term otherwise it was a half bottle of wine and quarter bottle of port.

I'm sure the importance of what you wear has gone by the way now. The women don't have to wear black. At that stage there were only a few of us in the hall. Quite often I would be the only woman. Suddenly, five years after I left, a lot of women started doing law. There were a lot of women doing solicitors. Now, I'm sure it's half and half.

I remember the food was execrable. Fair end of lamb. You couldn't smoke in the room and you couldn't drink coffee, because someone stole the cream jug. At the end of the meal a man would go around with snuff.

I took snuff. I took everything that was available, port, wine and snuff. If you wanted to leave the room to go to the loo you had to petition the benchers at the top of the room. They were long benches with barristers at them and you had to send them up a little note, 'Ms Donnelly *craves* that she may go to the Ladies' Room.'

Sometimes they'd be feeling very grudging and they'd say, 'No.' The little note would go up on a silver tray and then be returned in the same manner. The man who did the beer would also do this. I've forgotten his name but he was a lovely man. He wore a suit and breeches and carried the snuff around in a little silver dish. It was Daniel O'Connell's snuff dish, I think.

You were thrown out on the roadside, pissed, at half past seven. Then we all went to a pub down the road. It should have been called King's Inns Bar but it wasn't. It was at the end of Henrietta Street, which is such a beautiful street. It was quite extraordinary because a lot of the women from Moore Street drank in this pub. It was a totally matriarchal situation. It was Irish society turned on its head. Under normal circumstances you would have supposed it to be a huge pub full of men. Occasionally a man would enter very diffidently and his wife might buy him a drink or give him a pound. At this stage the men were at home looking after the children, because they didn't work. These women had inherited their stalls in Moore Street. They were fantastic, they'd been in business for generations.

At first they eyed us with a certain degree of mistrust. We got talking and eventually as time passed, a year passed and another and you're still there, three years and you got to know them. They were pretty marvellous, they really were.

There was one elderly woman and she had several adopted children. She lived in Henrietta Street and she was such a strong personality, straight as a die. It was a great start in life for the children for they were much loved and very indulged. They ran a really tight business and were proud of what they did, and rightly so.

They worked hard from a very early age and the pub was their relaxation. It was nice to see but I can assure you they weren't sitting around talking about fashion or what the milkman said. But the little diffident visits of the men were very funny.

I didn't finish the Inns because my father died. He was delighted he was going to have a daughter who was going to be a barrister. I didn't feel it was a very suitable job for me to do even though those years were great fun. I left and went to work for John Ryan who was publishing a literary magazine called the *Dublin Magazine* and I worked out in his house.

He was a fascinating and talented man in a whole range of areas. A gifted artist and writer, with a fantastic sense of judgement. He discovered a number of writers and encouraged others. He knew a lot about the sea. A real renaissance man, although that's a cliche. His interests are so varied and yet he's talented in so many of them.

The magazine lasted many years prior to my arrival but I think I killed it off. It used to come out quarterly; summer, autumn, winter and spring. While I was there there was an edition which contained three seasons in one. I was the editorial assistant. I kept pleading with him to make me an assistant editor which he very wisely resisted. I wasn't even a very good editorial assistant.

He was in the midst of writing *A Bash in the Tunnel*, his memoirs. He was very much a part of that scene which predated me. The Catacombs, Gainor Crist — the Ginger Man, Paddy Kavanagh, Brendan Behan and all these people who were

quite fascinating. I used to proof-read the typescript. Now that is something for which I have absolutely no talent, and weeping authors used to ring me up with work which had been honed for five years and each word a gem, a jewel and it would all have been reduced to this gobbledegook that I had proof-read. They were quite nice about it, although they couldn't believe it.

It wasn't a very lucrative way of living and I wanted to leave home. So eventually I just left and got a job in a travel agent of all things. When I left I lived in Rathmines, in Leinster Square in a flat which I didn't pay rent for. It belonged to friends of mine and they were very generous. They thought they were giving it to me for a fortnight but three years later I was still there.

In the early 70s Rathmines was terrific. Nowadays it's not, because the shops aren't open all the time. Then you could buy a rasher on Christmas Day in Rathmines. I was hideously poor. I used to go down to the Banba Bookshop and sell off, bit by bit, all my books. I worked three nights in this travel agents until they fired me. But there wasn't anything unpleasant in it. It simply became incumbent on them to get rid of me.

Meanwhile, I had a lot of friends who worked in advertising. I never saw it as a career for myself even though I had done some writing. That year I had had a story published in *Over 21* and another story in *Young Irish Writing*. I'd also had some execrable poetry published in the *Dublin Magazine*. It often comes back to haunt me and I've never seen anything so nauseating. I'm sure everybody has some poetry at home, they just don't put it in print.

It didn't occur to me that anyone wrote advertising. At that point I went to work in ARKS. It was the place to work and I was very lucky to get in there. It was situated at the top of Harcourt Street. Anyone, who was anyone, worked there at the time. I just couldn't believe that there would be very talented people who were so quick and fast. They were so quicksilvery, I couldn't understand what they were saying it seemed so clever and so fast.

I found it really exciting from the word go. I loved it. I loved writing the ads. The quickness was the pay-off. You didn't have to labour for nine long years for someone to recognise you. You wrote it at nine o'clock and someone loved it at ten. Or hated it!

I find it very hard to leave Dublin when I'm going to other cities and I give out when I come back. I hate the feeling of being under threat. I mean when we were young you got pissed and you walked 'till four in the morning. You were safe. I wouldn't walk at 5.30 in the evening now in certain parts of the city and I don't know what to do about it. You can't live on the dole and so you go out and hit someone over the head with a hammer.

I have an enormous affection for Dublin now, I get cross with it less often than other people. It's such a beautiful city, it's so seductive. It's insidious, it just creeps up on you. I feel that, all the time. I don't feel embittered by the things that happen in the city, I feel bitter about the tax system and the awful mistakes we have made, and God knows, we have done everything within our power to destroy our city.

Still overriding all are the Liberties, looking out at the Pigeon House, walking along Grafton Street and suddenly looking up and seeing all the buildings high up. Up in the car park in Drury Street you look out at the skyline and what you see is a beautiful city.

Clare Boylan

I was born in 1948 and lived in Terenure on Ashdale Road. What I remember most about that street is that there were no country people on it at all. There was a fair mixture of Catholics and Protestants. When I was growing up nearly every family I knew was a 'half and half'. Although outwardly mixed marriages were considered rather a disgrace, on both sides, and something that couldn't be done, it obviously could be done because we all had Protestant relations. Everyone seemed to have them, and the street was an even mix.

Round the corner from us was Ashdale Gardens, which was entirely Jewish. It was a street which had recently been built. Certainly the Jews had very recently come to it. Everybody seemed to be good neighbours and well accepted, although there was a certain wariness towards the Jews.

At one stage when I was growing up, I was about five or six, a country family came to live on the street. They had a lot of children which nobody else on the street had. There were six or seven and a lot of noise. I distinctly remember that they were the outsiders. They were not accepted. Everybody moved around together, Jews, Protestants and Catholics but the country people were not accepted. In some subtle way this communicated itself to us children, in that we slightly kept them at arm's length. We wouldn't let them join in our games and even made fun of them a little bit.

I'd a very protected childhood, so I didn't have that much of an independent life. We went round everywhere with my mother. Dublin to me as a child was Bewley's. The bookshops were also very central and the small shops in James' Street and Kevin Street. I always thought of them as second hand shops but they can't have been.

My mother used to do hospital visiting to old folk in St James' Street Hospital and it was a great treat for us children. The old ladies were always very vulgar. If they had their dinner out in front of them on a tray, they'd say, 'Ah that's lovely, the meat's so tender you could eat it with the cheeks of your arse.' The Legion of Mary, whom they hated, used to visit them, they were so polite and they would never bring anything to drink. There was one old lady called Joanna who always had her Baby Power and the Legion visitors would come around and pick it up and say, 'What have you got in your bottle, Joanna?' She'd answer with the utmost belligerence, 'Lourdes water.' They were very virtuous in those days.

It was a long walk from James' Hospital to the bus. We'd be in and out of all the little shops buying sweets. Certainly they sold second hand comics which was a great treat. I don't know how much they were. I think a comic was sixpence new and about a penny second hand. We'd be allowed to buy loads of sweets and comics. I always thought the sweets were second hand as well as the comics. They might well have been.

Bewley's was always the follow up to anything unpleasant. If you had to go to a doctor or the dentist you always went to Bewley's afterwards for a cream bun. I remember Bewley's with a mixture of delight and dread. It always meant some gruesome forerunner. But then you got your treat. I particularly loved the trifle they did in the paper case with chocolate shavings on top.

The pantomime at Christmas was always a very central part of a Dublin childhood. People like Jimmy O'Dea and Maureen Potter were world class movie stars as far as we were concerned. All the rest of the pantomime would be forgotten in the excitement of seeing them.

One year I couldn't see in the seat I was in. I suppose I was about four and the adults let me sit on the steps so I could get a better view. Some woman, in the dark, whom I couldn't see had a box of Black Magic chocolates that she kept handing me. That was the most magical thing. This invisible woman with her invisible hand giving me chocolates in the dark. I never saw who she was.

Another thing was Bushy Park in Terenure and you weren't allowed to go there because apparently it was full of dirty old men. This was an object of the greatest fascination — the dirty old men. We didn't know what dirty meant, whether they were just begrimed or what. Anyway it was a dreadful thing.

I had a younger cousin and we were always getting into scrapes together. I was always very well behaved because there were so few of us — only three, and my parents could keep an eye on us. I did what I was told. But once I got in with the cousin things changed. One day we got home late and my mother was ready to kill us, my cousin instantly said, 'Oh we met a dirty old man and we were chased by him and we had to hide.' My mother believed every word of it. 'Right children,' she said. 'He'll probably be coming this way.' She took us into the drawing room, the one we used on Christmas day and never used at any other time of year. We hid behind the curtains and she said, 'Nothing will happen to you, no one will give out to you. If you see the dirty man I want you to point him out to me.' So we stood there for hours and eventually some poor old fellow came along on his bicycle and my cousin, getting bored and wanting to go home, roared, 'There he is.' My mother flew out and hurled abuse at him and told him he'd be locked up for a hundred years. I always remember him wobbling off his bike, knowing he hadn't a chance if anyone came out after him. I had a great relish for bad company.

My other sisters all had friends who were identical types of children. We went to a national school, the Presentation Convent in Terenure. I was terribly spoilt as I was the youngest. My sisters used to tell me about the dreadful things that would happen when I went to school. I'd get beaten with chair legs and blood would pour out of me, supposedly. I don't know why, but I was never the least bit nervous or apprehensive about it. At my first day in school there was an old teacher called Miss Byrne, who was also a Dubliner, and as I came in the door expecting to be hit by the chair leg, she picked me up and kissed me and said, 'Ah, another little Boylan.'

I was put beside a girl called Annie who was poor and people were really very, very poor at that time in Dublin. Those, like us, who hadn't a penny but always had enough to eat saw them as a novelty. We never saw them as underprivileged. A novelty because they had milk and corned beef sandwiches at school and the nuns used to give them presents. Most unlikely things like gilded dried flowers that had had their day. I don't know what the beleaguered mothers of twelve did with these offerings. But it seemed to me, at the time, that they had all the advantages and privileges.

One girl from an 'underprivileged' family showed me how the ink-well worked and how you could take it out, stick your fingers up through it and down through the hole in the ink-well. We could have a war if she was on one side of the desk and I was on the other. She could poke her fingers up and I could poke mine down and nobody would know. We could be stabbing each other to death. I thought she was highly attractive. I then picked up, as my very best pal, another 'underprivileged girl' called Frankie.

Frankie had a great assortment of horse's teeth and she was very cheeky. I thought she was wonderful. I went around everywhere with her. I knew my mother didn't like her but would never, in a million years, say, 'She's the wrong sort of child. Stick with your own class.' She couldn't say it, so she waited for a specific flaw to show itself. Frankie used to call for me every day to go to school. I was always late. One of the things I loved about Frankie, and I couldn't correlate, was that, underprivileged and all as she was, she always had loads of money and she could buy sweets and apples on the way to school.

Then my mother discovered that Frankie, who also picked up a few other little girls on the way, pinched all the money from the pockets of the coats on the hall stand. Every house she went to, she'd arrive early and wait and then rifle all the coats in the hall. Mother was delighted — as she had an excuse to ban Frankie. That was the end of that friendship.

We weren't a house of readers, as a result I've missed out on a lot of things that I'll never catch up on. But we were absolutely besotted by bookshops. Fred Hanna's used to have a trestle table on the ground floor with bargain books on it, and under that, on the floor, were piled the super bargains, Lithuanian bibles and things. We'd spend hours there and get ourselves covered in muck. All Christmas shopping was done there. The grown ups bookshelves would be full of the most turgid stuff that nobody would ever read. The more turgid the look of the book the better the bargain. So for twopence you'd get the most enormous ghastly book and drag it home and give it to your parents. I don't know what became of them. I'm sure Fred Hanna was delighted to have them removed.

We went to the pictures about three times a week, which I think most families in Dublin did. It didn't matter what was on — that was life, just to go to the pictures. We went to the Classic and the Kenilworth. I remember the lovely brass staircase in the Stella.

I loved going to Sandymount on my holidays. I knew every inch of it. We took my grandparents' house and they would go to Bray. Bray was a great expedition, the grand tour. When we went out to visit them the adults would go off for a drink and we'd be given a half crown each to go down to Albert's Walk. They had the cheapest juke boxes and all the slot machines were there, so we had great value for our two and six.

I loved the theatre and from a very early age I thought I would love to go on stage. I only had the bare bones of experience when we entered a school drama competition. I was fourteen. It was the Irish drama competition and it was on in Damer Hall. I was playing a bride. The wrong costume arrived, a tutu instead of a long wedding dress. It had to be padded out with all sorts of frilly slips. All the other competitors were boys and as I stood there trying to say my few lines in Irish they all shouted, 'Get them off,' for the whole performance. We won every award in sight. Best play, best actress, best costume, we won them all.

That was the end of acting for me. I always loved the theatre and money, although I never had any of that. At the age of fourteen I formed myself and my sisters into a pop group. They had no choice or input into the project at all. I was the organiser and the manager and I was the number three singer. I can hold a note but I certainly can't sing. Anyway we formed this group and we called ourselves the Girlfriends. In those days the cinemas were beginning to close down. They weren't closing to become pool halls or bingo halls, they were becoming variety shows. The Apollo Cinema in Sundrive, and another Apollo in Crumlin and what had been the Plaza and was then the Cinerama, they all became variety shows.

Guys like Chris Casey were the big stars. The act consisted of him dressing up as a woman and taking two cabbages out of his jumper as the grand finale of his act. This was about the height of it. We got a spot in the Variety shows and first of all we got ten shillings a week. Then it went up to thirty shillings. It was great. It gave us ten bob each.

I went to St Louis in Rathmines. I didn't do the Leaving there, I did it in Rathmines Tech because I discovered that I could do it there in a year. I had given up any idea of the stage at that time, but I was still keen on some sort of stage work. I thought I'd become a writer. Rathmines Tech was great then. The age group was from thirteen to thirty. It was full of misfits and drop outs and ex-priests and there was a real 'Educating Rita' girl there. Her name was Sheila and she'd no education whatsoever. She'd gone off to work in a factory in Birmingham when she was fourteen. She was about twenty-five when she decided to come back and start all over again. There was a great atmosphere in the class as a result. There were a lot of fellas, as well, from upper middle class backgrounds. The teachers were wonderful. Their idea was not to get you to pass exams but to get as much as possible out of you.

They did everything to develop your confidence and they never laughed at you. Two of the teachers decided to set up a paperback library. They brought in a number of bound books under a special import license. We all had to give threepence to keep the library going and everyone of us was to take out one book. It could be anything you liked. It could be *The Joy of Sex*, it could be a western or Proust. You could take what you wanted. But we had special two hour classes in which you had to stand up and talk about what we had read. Initially the boys took out the most rubbishy books they could find, but when they stood up to discuss them they felt like idiots, and when the others would stand up and talk about books they thought were stuffy, they'd suddenly find that they were interesting. They'd want to read them. We all got a tremendous reading background in a year.

140

I wrote a few poems that year, I was at that age. One of the teachers encouraged me and I got a poem published and that decided me to become a writer.

My first job when I left school was in Eason's. I went to so much trouble for the customers, tearing up parcels in the wholesale to see what book had come in and looking up the catalogue numbers. No one has ever done that for me in there. Eason's was a real Dublin place. The girls in there were real Dublin and the discussion in the canteen at the break was who had had a rub of the relic. I was absolutely shocked by this talk. They were great. I didn't last that long because the work was so blooming hard. But while I was there I made use of the fact that there were magazine stands. I read all the magazines I could lay my hands on to see what they published. I sent stories off to them and that was really how I started.

I think that when we were growing up, although we weren't great readers, there was more of a naturally cultural environment. There was no Concert Hall then but people went to the opera or the theatre or the circus. They went out a fair bit and they discussed a lot.

My grandfather was knocked down and killed on his way to the circus, when he was ninety. He was a man who constantly went to every kind of entertainment and enjoyed it. He was an opera singer. In his early youth he sang with Count John McCormack. When he was in his eighties somebody told him that Gigli was on in town. He was incredibly excited because he loved Gigli. He was asked if he wanted to go and he said, 'Oh lovely that would be wonderful.' Of course his hearing wasn't the best and it turned out that it wasn't Gigli at all, it was the film Gigi. 'Ah sure it was lovely anyway,' he said. He enjoyed it just as much.

Dublin was never really Venice for opera, where the audience would shout their heads off, as if they were at a soccer match. In Dublin you knew that if they hadn't liked the opera they would throw eggs or tomatoes at the performers. It wasn't that they knew opera, simply that they listened to it and rejoiced in it.

Dubliners had a great vulgar sense of humour. They still have. I think it's marvellous. But they were a very discreet people, never asked questions about money, didn't ask direct questions. The other side of that I suppose is that they minded their own business a bit too much. Apart from the centre of Dublin there probably wasn't much of a community spirit. But I think there's a feeling of invasion now. That feeling of privacy and natural gentility and delicacy has been invaded. It could be the level of bureaucracy. People just seem to talk about politics and money all the time.

Certainly this would not have been done in my time. It would have been considered really bad form. You told a few stories and you sang a few songs and you pretended things weren't serious. It's got a bit dull now, heavy handed and self-conscious. A lot's been lost.

From what I remember when I was growing up there wasn't any money, and there were never any clothes bought. My parents never seemed to say, 'Her shoes are worn down,' or, 'Her dress is worn out. What are we going to do?' If there was a communion, a confirmation, or a school uniform needed, then the money was found. But other than that there were never any clothes bought.

We used to go to the Iveagh Market with our pocket money. When we got there, instead of buying a nice cotton dress, we'd buy floor length silk nightdresses and evening dresses smelling of moth balls. They were so irresistible. The smell was terrible but the clothes were wonderful. We loved the Iveagh Market.

I was at a dinner recently in the newly restored Pillar Room in the Rotunda Hospital. It is wonderful. Anything that sees a resurrection of the beautiful Dublin that was, the solid ornate lovely Dublin, anything to do with that is a triumph.

The Millennium seems to be a concentrated effort to divert from the depression of people who haven't enough money to live on and who have no jobs. If money allocated for the Millennium was put, instead, towards the preservation or restoration of parts of Dublin, then I would feel it was a much more sincere endeavour.

I mean, it will all be over in a year anyway.

Geraldine Murphy

I was born in Ballybough on the north side of the city, one of a family of eight. When I was four years old we moved to an old tenement in Eccles Street, opposite the Mater Hospital. There were two tenements and we lived in number 45, up in the front drawing room. About eight other families were living in that house. One of my earliest memories, and the one that has always stayed with me, is of the family that lived on the landing beside us, in the back drawingroom, a family of five children and the mother and father.

The mother of the family died of consumption and on the night of her wake there was the bombing of Dublin. I will never forget the Air Raid Precaution men coming up the street, shouting up at everybody to turn off the lights in their rooms. They told us the bombing was going on and we could feel the vibrations as the bombs dropped on the Phoenix Park and on the North Strand. Everyone in the house, men, women and children, had to come down into the room where the woman was being waked. I will always have the memory of her lying there on the bed, as though on a bier. I suppose it was a brass bed but it looked like a bier to me. That's where we had to spend the night, terrified. I was petrified that the bomb was going to come into the room. Of course, a lot of the people at the wake had plenty of drink taken and they didn't pay a blind bit of attention to the order to switch off the lights. Anyway, didn't the vibrations shake the corpse in the bed and her mouth fell open and a prayer book had to be shoved under her chin to close it again.

There was also a prostitute from Scotland living in that house and my mother had great sympathy for her. Nobody in the house seemed too concerned at her profession and in fact, on the night of the bombing she was missing and everyone was worried about her, wondering if she was alright. Then she was prosecuted and was to appear in court, but she didn't turn up. The police came to the house looking for her and when they couldn't get any answer at her door, they got ladders and climbed up to her window, but she was out. Eventually they caught up with her and she was deported. The welfare officer who was dealing with her case told my mother that when the boat docked she was missing. No one knows what happened to her, whether she threw herself overboard, slipped through the net or met up with a sailor.

We moved to Mountjoy Street when I was ten years old. My mother had been left a little money and could afford to buy a house. They were very cheap at that time. It was very pleasant living there, in that big wide street, with little or no traffic and plenty of room to play street games.

When I was about eighteen years old, I got involved in the Legion of Mary and we used to do a visitation around the tenements in Dominic Street and the area around Mountjoy Street. We also visited those huge houses in Henrietta Street. They fascinated us because you could get lost in them. Some of them had two staircases, housing as many as twenty families.

Even though we were on a religious exercise, we couldn't help but notice the poverty and lack of facilities that the people had to endure. They had to go from the top to the bottom of those houses to use a communal lavatory and some of the basements with families in them, were in a deplorable state.

The city has changed an awful lot since I was a teenager. Part of our recreation was walking into the city, particularly at night time, rambling around, looking into the shops. It was a great pastime. Nowadays it's all shuttered up at night. On the days when there was a football match, there was an air of innocent excitement up and down O'Connell Street. It was a safe place to be in. We used to walk home from the dances at one or two o'clock in the morning and we weren't a bit afraid. There was less traffic, too. We used to go a lot to the films because it was cheap. You could get into the Savoy for only sixpence. Now there seems to be an awful lot of people around and it's very noisy. It's very smelly, as well, and you can feel the pollution, even in your mouth.

In 1965, I got married and went down to live off Pearse Street, in Queen's Terrace. My husband had lived there all his life, in one of the little cottages. He was always interested and involved in politics and eventually I was influenced to the extent that I began to notice things around me that I hadn't been aware of before and I began to see things in a different light.

I had always worked, but after my son was born, I was in and around the area more. It was then I began to see the problems facing women with children; the difficulties in simply trying to cross a road, of having to get off the footpath because of parked cars and there didn't seem to be many places for children to play.

Noel Browne, at that time, was busy preparing for an election. I had read a lot about him and I admired him greatly. When he started agitating for the opening of Merrion Square to the public, I attended some of the public meetings on this issue. Only residents of the square, who had keys, were entitled to use it. These meetings brought me into contact with other people in the area and I became more and more involved in local issues.

A retreat was held in Westland Row and the priest went around talking to the people. He discovered that their main worry was housing, because so many of the neighbours were being shunted off out to the suburbs, to places like Ballymun, Ballyfermot and Crumlin.

As the people were being moved out, the developers were moving in. Walking up Mount Street, you'd see all these derelict spaces, houses standing with their roofs gone. We worried about what was going to happen. A lot of traditional firms, that had given employment in the area, seemed to be in places that had become run down. The upshot of the peoples' fear and worry was the setting up of an organisation called The Community Council, to keep an eye on what was happening and to find out what planning applications, and so on, were being sought in the area.

At this time there was already a very good active committee down in City Quay which had been agitating to have local authority houses built in the area. Professional people, such as architects and solicitors, had been giving them a hand. They rolled in behind us and through meetings and talks, we eventually set up an exhibition. The architects and students from University College Dublin (UCD) helped us to draw out a plan of our area, which was bounded by Harmony Row, Macken Street and Pearse Street.

The exhibition was held in St. Andrew's Community Centre, in Pearse Street, and was funded by The Arts Council, around about 1975-76. It demonstrated the type of housing we wanted in the area for the future and it was very well received. It was a hundred years of looking back at City Quay, at its activities, its people and the type of jobs they had.

The publicity it received was very favourable and extensive. A lot of higher officials in the corporation came to have a look at it and were very impressed.

It gave a great deal of confidence to the people in the area and to The Community Council and as a result we were better able to put forward our ideas when we went on deputations to Dublin Corporation.

When the Compulsory Purchase Order was put on Queen's Terrace, we knew we would have to move, even though we didn't want to. We had hoped that the corporation would build the new houses gradually and then move the people from the old into the new as they became available. That way, we could all have stayed in the area and the community would have remained intact.

That didn't happen but we did gain one advantage. The corporation had to move the majority of us to the new houses in Ringsend and although it took us a long time to acclimatise, we felt that we had got a better deal than most. Looking now at our new environment, most of us are satisfied living in Ringsend. The new houses which were built in Hoban Place and Queen's Terrace, were greatly appreciated by everyone.

Now that the housing needs of the people had been met, even though only partially, we had to look and see what other problems needed to be tackled. The Social Services Council was expanding its scope to help people with social problems and to help the elderly. We saw there was another role for a body that could do research into the general needs of the area and so we had an AnCO sponsored survey on jobs and unemployment.

We found that many of the traditional jobs were dying away. Industries, which had generations of families working in them, were being relocated in new industrial estates. There was very little employment for women because they had gone in for sewing and hotel work and many of the hotels had closed down and the sewing factories had moved out.

The area was full of office blocks and as our young people had never been trained to work in them we decided to set up a secretarial course. The IDA was developing its industrial complex down in Pearse Street at this time. We knew they would be relocating industries from other parts of the city and would be bringing their own staff with them. We had been promised that these firms would expand and employ local people but it didn't happen to the extent we had

Lucy Johnston

147

been promised. We made representations to the management of the complex to tease out the idea of us setting up our own co-ops and they were very agreeable and helpful, as was AnCO and the Youth Employment Agency.

We set up a restaurant and a secretarial co-op but unfortunately the restaurant didn't succeed. Some of the reasons for its closure were our own, but a lot were outside our control. We had it for a year and during that time we trained about ten young people and we employed a chef and a manager. The secretarial co-op did very well, though, and this year we are into a profit situation.

In Westland Row we have a Voluntary Housing Association and we are able to house newly married people for two years to start them off. We have a savings scheme built into the rent. I'd like to see more flexibility in the type of housing we have, more mixed co-operative housing.

I hope that in this year of the Millennium, the focus will be on local communities and their environments. In the Westland Row and Pearse Street area, there are a number of vacant sites, some of them in public ownership. These should be developed, with the needs of the local communities as a priority.

An Bord Gáis now owns the Gas Company site in Pearse Street and the Westland Row Community Council wishes to see it developed to accommodate multi purpose usage with low cost family housing (both local authority and co-operative) with industry and business that the local people could benefit from. I believe that communities should be allowed a say and have an input into new developments planned for their areas.

Maureen Potter

I was born in Ballybough. A friend called Mrs Porter had what they would call a nursing home and I was born there. I was brought home to number six Philipsburg, or as everyone says, Phyllisburg Avenue, Fairview. It's right behind the Visitation Church. On the Philipsburg Avenue was Saint Mary's National School which had five rooms and three classes to each room. That was extraordinary. To have arithmetic going on in one corner and Irish in another and English in another.

I found it great, because when I later went to dancing school I used to nick out of school before time and go to the Queen's. That's gone now, and it was a lovely little theatre. It was very handy to swop places with kids all along the line and drop underneath and be gone. And then to come in the next day to face remarks like, 'Oh so the little princess is back . . . So you deign to join us again, Miss Potter.'

My father was a commercial traveller for the Vacuum Oil Company. Consequently we had a car which was rather nice and he had a driver because he had hurt his legs and couldn't drive anymore. So we thought we were a little posh, but we weren't. We were just like everyone else on the Terrace.

We had lovely neighbours. There were five Deady sisters and one brother, who lived two doors down. There were lovely little houses, with only two bedrooms, in Joseph's Terrace. You could build on a bathroom if you wanted to at the back. Indeed I wouldn't mind one now.

The Miss Deadys used to give us pear sweets, which actually smelled like fruit. When you ate a pear drop you would practically be eating a pear. I had two brothers, we were the only children living on the Terrace, a row of six houses, and we'd go up to Miss Deadys' house and knock on the door hoping to God they were in. One of them always was. What fascinated me then, and paralyses me now, was their stuffed peacock. I have never seen the like in my life, not even in the museum with all those dinosaurs. There in the little hall was this bloody big thing, which you had to squeeze past.

Their house had all kinds of scents and smells of cooking and French perfume because one of the Miss Deadys was a governess in France, in Paris. She came home about twice a year and we used to wait for her to arrive. She would come like something out of a 1930s film, like Claudette Colbert, wearing a little cloche hat, always in black and white or navy and white. We'd be out there with our mothers and my mother would say, 'Ohhhhhh lovely, look at that. That's Paris, France, isn't it lovely?'

Up the road lived the Murphy sisters. Two of them were murdered in the little shop in Ballybough where they lived.

Then my father died. He went into hospital to have his leg removed in 1932 and, in those days, without the antibiotics that we have now, he died of pneumonia. So that was that. No more sixpences on a Sunday for *The Magnet* and *The Gem* with Billy Bunter and *The Hotspur* and *The Wizard* and *The Rover*. These were the English comics.

My mother used to buy my clothes in 'Our Boys' shop. It was easier to get jumpers and overcoats there and I'd be substituted with a skirt.

When Daddy died everything was gone. No car, no insurance or anything. The house changed ownership. A lovely family called Cullen owned the houses originally. In fact one of them, Maureen Cullen became my godmother. She married a guard and they moved out to Dundrum. I saw her a couple of years ago after about forty years. The houses were sold to Doctor Barnes from Duleek who very kindly gave us another house. It was fabulous, just opposite the Terrace. The Gordons used to have it and it was called Mulberry Lodge and Charles Lever once lived there. It was heaven. It wasn't posh, because the house was so old. I don't know if we paid rent or not, but we lived in this magnificent old house, with an actual mulberry tree in the garden. If you climbed up high enough in the tree you could see over it into the school yard next door. That's why I hadn't much chance of not going to school, though I managed it a couple of times.

We always had cats and rabbits. We also kept pigeons and we built a house for them. It blew down one day in a storm and they all flew away. My brothers were great for animals. We used to bring them in and give them Peg Legs and nurse them. We had a black rat which died and I put him in the harmonium in school, and was a heroine for taking it out. No one else would touch it and when the smell got too much and everyone said, 'What's that?' I said, 'I'll have a look Miss,' and took it out. My rat. I put it in the bin and everyone said, 'Bravo, Maureen.' First decent thing I'd ever done at school, the first right thing.

I remember gathering berries for mulberry jam. You could make mulberry jam then. It was the only time I tasted mulberry jam. We used to come down out of the tree like wine coloured savages. All the neighbours would be sending messages into my mother, 'Keep them kids out of the tree. Their clothes are being ruined.'

There were lots of families in Philipsburg Avenue at the time. Macintoshes across the way, the Bolgers, the Woodrows and the Bennets and they're all gone now. They're all flats now. But they were lovely old houses with lovely long gardens. The Macintoshes, or the Miss Macs, lived in Merton Hall. One of them used to teach dancing in a hut at the end of the garden. We all used to go in there for dances at night, with just the piano and drums.

In 1935 I went to work for Jimmy O'Dea. Prior to this I went to the Connie Ryan school of dancing after being to Dewy Byrne's school of dancing, in the CYMS in Phyllisburg Avenue, Fairview. Miss Byrne, a lovely woman, thought I had outgrown her school and recommended me to Connie Ryan, who took me over. It was great. She used to teach the O'Dea girls, you know, Jimmy O'Dea's dancers, and she was also a soubrette, as they called them then, out in the front doing the high kicks and singing, 'I'm goin' back to Inverary,' and all sorts of Scottish songs that had nothing to do with anything.

We'd work in extraordinary places like the Esplanade. We'd get the tram up from Ballybough to the old Esplanade where they held the Carnivals up by Collins Barracks, at Kingsbridge. The Esplanade was a great place, famous for its merry-go-rounds. In the tent they had competitions for dancing and singing and I always came away with something. All the mothers would say, 'That's not fair! She's a professional. She's goin' to Connie Ryan. She's been on the Royal. That's not fair. Don't give it to that one . . .' You know the usual.

But we went to do this little show in the Star Cinema, Bray which is no longer there. Jimmy O'Dea came along to see the show and he put me in a pantomime in the Olympia in 1935. That is when I used to see the sunburst of the Bovril advertisement, there at the corner of D'Olier Street and Westmoreland Street. I played Alfie Byrne, who was the great Lord Mayor at the time. Jimmy O'Dea got a lovely little suit made for me, but he used to keep losing the moustache and we'd find it on the sole of my shoe, and there'd be bloody murder. That was my first professional job.

My father was a lovely man. He was about six feet two but my mother was only my height. He was musical. We made our own entertainment, and of course, they always made their own crystal sets. My dad was always experimenting with crystal sets and Henry Hall would come over loud and clear.

The church organist was a man called George Crehan, and we had a friend called Dodo Dermody. Isn't that a lovely name? My aunt Eileen was a wanderer and went all over the world. When she'd come home my mother would play the piano and someone else would play the fiddle.

My mother once sang on a platform with Count John McCormack. She was a member of a Quartet and she was taught by Esposito. She had the chance of a couple of lessons from this Esposito and won a few gold medals for singing. So on Sunday night all you could hear was the piano and the violin and my mother singing *One alone to be my own* and us creeping down from the one bedroom, hanging over the banisters, listening and waiting to see if there'd be anything left in the glasses for us to drink, which we did. One morning we went into the parlour, as it was known then, with the piano and the occasional tables and the good lamp and we tried out the dregs of Guinness. Well, never again. I'll never forget the smell, and I'll never forget the smell of the tea leaves my mother used to spread to keep down the dust. No such things as vacuum cleaners then.

Now that was a real Monday morning smell in our house. Also the washing with the smell of the Sunlight soap. We didn't have washing powder in those days. The Sunlight was sliced into the boiling water and allowed to soften, until it was ready to put the clothes in. A lovely woman called Maggie used to help on a Monday morning with the huge big tub, but the smell would drive you absolutely out of your mind.

I'd say we were very comfortable. I remember my father bringing home a man called Uncle Kit who stayed for a year. My father used to bring all sorts of people home when he'd return on Friday night. No one ever found out Uncle Kit's other name. He used to eat and go out and come home and then he left. That was the sort of thing they did then.

My father used to play poker on Friday night with the lads when he came home. George Crehan would be there and he became the musical director (MD) in the old Olympia. A lovely man. His brother was Richard Crehan who was the MD in the London Palladium in the 1930s. We all thought this was marvellous. In the old days the MD was very important. He was very well known in England.

We were living in old Mulberry Lodge which was lovely because it had all sorts of little corners and it had a conservatory with a vine that had grapes. This house was an adventure, everything you could imagine, little secret cupboards and little odd shaped corners.

I was the tree, the candle on the first birthday of the Theatre Royal Birthday Cake and I stood at the top of it, this huge tree. It was made up of girls as slices rather like Busby Berkeley. Slices coming away and me singing, 'Many happy returns,' at the top of my voice because there was no microphone. But it worked.

I did a lot of work with Jimmy Campbell and Jack Hylton and the manager of the Royal, Dick McGrath. He got me an audition with Jack Hylton's Band. He was huge at the time. I went up to his room in the Royal, the huge number one. He had his grand piano and I did my bit. He was delighted with me and put me on that Saturday night. He introduced me, 'And now we 'ave one of yer own, one of yer own little girls who's made good, *Muriel* Potter.'

So I did the act and then I forgot all about him. I went away on holidays to Portmarnock with my cousin Joan. We decided to make chocolate one day with the bunsen burner and burnt down half the house. My aunt Eily was out at the time. Of course Joan being the very brave girl she was, marvellous in any adversity, put out the fire with all my clothes. Not one of her own, MINE!!! So I'd nothing. I remember going out and sitting in a barrel, a rain barrel. I'd no clothes, nothing.

Then a telegram came from Jack Hylton, and me with no clothes, 'Come at once. Two months to broadcast in BBC.' So I borrowed a dress that came down to my ankles and a raincoat from somebody else. I went to Jack Hylton for two months and stayed for two years. I went all around Germany, Holland and England and Scotland. Peggy Dell was with me. She was a real Dubliner.

Then the war broke out on 3 September, 1939. We were in the London Palladium playing with Arthur Askey, Flanagan and Allen and all that Crazy Gang. Jack Hylton closed down and blacked out three days before the war broke out, the whole of London was blacked out. We were sent down to Blackpool to his mother and father to see if it would pass. On the Sunday morning we were sitting in Blackpool looking at this extraordinary empty beach with just rolls of barbed wire. I don't know how the English thought they were going to repel the Germans because all they had were these rolls of barbed wire, all along Blackpool beach. Everything else was bleak desolation and all the people were in their houses listening to the radio.

We went home and my mother said, 'Oh no.' I immediately joined Jimmy O'Dea at the Gaiety, this was something great. He used to play the Queen's in the twenties. In those days we still had the Royal and the Capitol. I was with O'Dea for a couple of years. He took off for England to broadcast in Bristol and there was nothing, no touring around the country. A very nice Englishman called Bob Johnson, who had been Jimmy O'Dea's stage manager, put a word in for me. He'd got a job at the Capitol, which was a beautiful theatre. It was built as an opera house and it was magnificent. That went overnight just like the Metropole

153

and the Queen's.

The Capitol did three shows a day. I went in there for one week and stayed eleven weeks. I worked regularly with Martin Crosbie and Thelma Ramsay. Thelma is one of my best friends. She does all my shows with me. They were the days when we had no English entertainers coming over.

I was away touring with Jimmy O'Dea when I heard about the bombs dropping on Fairview. When I returned I discovered that the side of Mulbery Lodge had collapsed as a result of the vibrations from the bomb. It was so old it just crumbled.

We moved out to Crumlin and what a change. The difference was great. In Philipsburg Avenue they were all older people and families who had been there for generations, but in Crumlin there were loads of kids our own age and we had great fun.

Barry Fitzgerald, 'the bishop-wouldn't-do-that-to-me', came over to see one of our shows, when Jimmy O'Dea was alive, in the Gaiety. He loved it. It was before we had the bar and the Green Room and all that posh stuff in the Gaiety and we only had a hatch, a little hole in the wall. He met me afterwards and he said, 'How are you?' and I said, 'I'm grand.' Then he said, 'Where do you live?' and I said, 'Fairview.' 'O Jesus, I haven't been in Fairview for years,' he said, and he a big star from Hollywood. So we got into a taxi and we toured Dublin and I showed him Winetavern Street and all around the Liberties.

Myself and Barry toured Dublin that night and for the whole of the trip he called me Maisie. I thought that was great. Maybe it was a premonition of the things to come, Maisie Madigan, fifty years later. I never thought I'd be in an Abbey play. An O'Casey play. I was thrilled to get the part. I was petrified but thrilled. I had no idea he wrote so beautifully. Shakespeare had nothing on Sean O'Casey. He has a saying for every situation in life. Absolutely magnificent.

I love Dublin, especially in the Autumn. There are still places and patches of Dublin that are absolutely lovely. If you go up towards Holles Street and around that area. Little areas in Ranelagh, Mount Pleasant, Fairview. You can still find a few of the old houses left on the corners if you turn into Melrose Avenue.

I don't like what's happening to my city. They've torn down some incredible buildings and monuments. I thought the blowing up of Nelson's Pillar was a disgrace. I don't know who could have cheered that. That was our history. People fought while that was there for their country. You might as well blow up Trinity College. I mean Elizabeth gave us that.

As for the Millennium, I think it's a marvellous idea. It's to attract tourists. It's also to give a sense of civic pride to us, the citizens of Dublin. At least I hope it does. I hope they include everybody in it. Not just the Liberties, which will be very prominent, but also the suburbs. Places like Tallaght, they're all Dubliners, moved from the inner city.

I remember cycling and getting caught up in the tram lines, it was incredible, I kept falling in front of motorists and being cursed from a height. I used to extricate myself and get into the Gaiety full of mud from Crumlin. The last time I used the bicycle I was going home to Crumlin and I turned round the corner into Pleasant Street, where the Olympic is. This will show you my age, I ran straight into an air raid shelter which had no light and which no one ever used. I ended up with an accordion under my arm and had to walk all the way to Crumlin with this bloody thing. I had no lights naturally enough. Baang. The bike telescoped just like that.

Then it was the bus but I still had to walk home. I used to walk miles. Do you remember those platform shoes, wooden, when the leather was a bit scarce. They had a sort of a hinge and if you walked in them too long your feet were burnt. We walked from Tallaght after a show with the late Johnny Brennan. And the terrible thing was that we had moved back to Fairview from Crumlin. It was when I'd met Jack first. If we'd still lived in Crumlin it wouldn't have been so bad. But we had to walk from Tallaght to Fairview. Jesus Mary and Joseph . . . We seemed to walk everywhere.

There was a woman who used to sing on O'Connell Bridge, 'Martha Mary Anne Magee she's a darlin, she 's a daisy and she's eyes that make you crazy,' and if you didn't give her something she'd roar at you.

There were other lovely women, there were two of them, two sisters. They used to sing inside the shops in Grafton Street. I never remember their names but they had a dog called Trixie. We became great friends and I used to steal bits of meat out of the theatre for Trixie.

They used to sing:

> 'Oh I want to be alone
> Oh I want to be alone
> Oh I want to be alone
> With Mary Brown
> If I meet her in the park
> I will get her in the dark
> And I'll tell her she's the sweetest girl in town.'

Oh I remember that. Do you remember that?

Biographical Notes

TINA BYRNE was born in 1961 and has lived all her life in Fatima Mansions. She left school at the age of 15 and worked in a meat factory and at the sewing. She is very actively involved in local issues and is the co-ordinator of the Environmental Programme in Fatima. At the moment she is working with the tenants in Fatima to ensure their participation in Dublin Corporation's Proposal Plan for Fatima Mansions.

STELLA WEBB is a retired solicitor. She is a member of the Religious Society of Friends and is an Executive Member of the committee which runs the Historical Library in Swanbrook, headquarters of the Quakers in Ireland. She is Vice-President of both the Irish United Nations Association and the Irish Campaign for Nuclear Disarmament.

CATHLEEN O'NEILL was born in the Liberties. During the late 1950s the family was rehoused in Ballyfermot while she was still a child but Cathleen always regarded the Liberties as her place. She lives in Kilbarrack where she has firmly taken root since her move there in her early adult life. She takes a keen interest in adult education and is organiser of a writers' group in Kilbarrack within KLEAR (Kilbarrack Local Education for Adult Renewal). Cathleen is deeply committed to and involved in all aspects of women's issues. She is currently designing women's poster for the Millennium and has received a grant for it from the Millennium Committee. The idea for the poster was Cathleen's.

ELLEN KENNEDY has lived all her life in York Street where she was born in 1926. She worked in a factory for a number of years but is now employed by the Combat Poverty Agency. Ellen is very much involved in her local area. She is Secretary of the Resident's Association and Whitefriar Youth Club. She is on the Parish Council of Whitefriar Street Chuch and is also on the Management Board of Whitefriar Street School.

PAULINE CUMMINS was born in 1949 and graduated from the National College of Art in 1969 where she specialised in painting and ceramics. She has taken part in many group shows in Ireland, the USA and Canada, including the Irish Exhibition of Living Art. She has been particularly active in exploring sensuality, sexuality, pregnancy and motherhood in her work. In 1986 Pauline Cummins was the recipient of the George Campbell Memorial Travel Award. At the moment she is Chairperson of Women Artists' Action Group.

ELAINE CROWLEY grew up in Clanbrassil Street in the late 1920s. She emigrated to England in 1945 at the end of the Second World War and joined the Auxiliary Training Services (ATS). After her marriage she lived abroad for some years then finally settled in Wales. She regularly returns to Dublin on holidays and to see her family. Eleven years ago she began writing and has had two best selling books published. The first, Dreams of Other Days is a novel set during the Great Famine and the second, A Man Made to Measure is a novel about her native Dublin during the time of the 1916 Rebellion. At the moment she is writing a sequel to Dreams of Other Days which follows the fortunes of some of the main characters who emigrated to America after the Famine.

TWINK, whose real name is Adele King, was born on the South Circular Road and grew up in Templeogue in the 1960s. She has been a professional entertainer since she was five years of age and has such a list of awards to her name that it would be impossible to mention them all in a short biography. She plays the part of Rosie in the new Pierce Brosnan movie Taffin, has two new series of Play The Game for 1988 and will be representing Ireland again in June in an international music festival in the south of Turkey.

DEIRDRE KELLY was born in 1938. She is an artist by profession having graduated from the

College of Art while it was still in Kildare Street. In the early 1960s she travelled alone through Russia, Hungary and Egypt, sleeping under canvas. Since the late 60s she has been involved in various issues in the city, including Hume Street, Wood Quay and road widening controversies. She is the author of two books *Hands Off Dublin* published in 1976 and *They are all out of step but our Corpo* published by the Living City Group. Deirdre also edited a monthly planning news-sheet *City Views* for four years between 1977-1981. In 1986 she was the co-ordinator of the very successful Dublin Crisis Conference which was held in the Synod Hall in Christ Church. At the moment she is the chairperson of the Living City Group.

NUALA O'FAOLAIN, born in Dublin in the 1940s, is a journalist with *The Irish Times*. She has lectured in English in UCD and NIHE. She has also worked as a television producer with RTE and the BBC. In 1986 she won a Jacob's Award for her TV series *Plain Tales* and in 1987 she received the prestigious award of Woman Journalist of the Year.

MURIEL McCARTHY was born in Dublin in the 1930s and at the moment holds the position of Librarian in Marsh's Library. She was also Librarian in Dr Worth's Library in Steeven's Hospital before its recent closure. She has been a member of the Old Dublin Society for a number of years and was President of the Society from 1981 to 1985. She was re-elected President in 1987. She holds an Honorary Degree from Trinity College, Dublin and was a recent recipient of the Lord Mayor's Millennium Award. Muriel McCarthy is also the author of *All Graduates and Gentlemen* a history of Marsh's Library published in 1980.

MARY MOONEY, born in 1958 in Meath Street in the Liberties, was elected to Dublin Corporation in 1985 and became one of the youngest aldermen ever. She contested the Dail elections in 1987 and won a seat. She is now the second youngest member of the Dail and represents Dublin South Central, a five seat constituency. When the road widening scheme for Clanbrassil Street was being voted on in the City Council before its final acceptance, Mary defied the party whip and voted against the scheme.

MARY BLACK grew up in Charlemont Street in the early 1960s and comes from a very musical family. A Contemporary Folk Singer, Mary has

been winning awards from an early age, the latest being the Irish Recorded Music Awards for the best Irish female vocalist which she has won two years in succession, in 1987 and 1988. She has just completed a two month tour of Ireland and is about to begin a three week tour of America. Her latest album *By the Time it Gets Dark* has gone platinum, having sold 25,000 since Christmas.

JONI CRONE was reared in Macken Street in the early 1950s. She was twelve when her family had to move out to Finglas. She has had a number of plays produced by the Raised Eyebrow Theatre Group of which she was a founder member. She is currently writing a novel and is active in feminist politics.

ELIZABETH GERAGHTY is a northside Dubliner born on City Quay in 1907. She comes from a republican and trade union background and was very active in both movements in her youth. She has vivid recollections of the early years of the trade union movement, the 1916 Rising and the Civil War and was well acquainted with many of the personalities involved.

JEAN ROCHE grew up in the 1950s in Benburb Street. She is a member of the National Executive Committee of the Communist Party of Ireland and is Chairperson of the Women's Committee. She is also assistant editor of the *Irish Socialist*. She has stood as a candidate in both local and national elections. She works in a tailoring factory.

JUNE LEVINE was born in Dublin and grew up in the Pembroke area in the early 1930s. At the age of six her family moved to the South Circular Road district. She is a writer and broadcaster and a founder member of the Irish Women's Liberation Movement. Her book *Sisters, A Personal Story of an Irish Feminist* was a bestseller. She is currently working on a novel set in India. She is co-author of the book *Lyn, A Story of Prostitution in Dublin* which headed the bestsellers' list for months.

EVELYN OWENS was a member of Seanad Eireann for eight years. During her last four years as a Senator she was the first women ever elected to the position of Leas-Cathaoirleach. She was also a former President of the Local Government and Public Service Union. Since 1984 she has been working full-time in the

Labour Court where she is the first woman to hold the position of Deputy Chairperson.

MARJORIE HAMPTON was born in Ranelagh and grew up in the early 1940s. She is very involved in the Cathedral affairs of St. Patrick's and is Secretary to Dean Griffin. She is also Vice President of Old Alexandra Hockey Club and runs a Keep Fit class in Rathmines.

EILEEN REID, the well-known Dublin singer was born and grew up in the Liberties in the 1950s. Between 1962 and 1968 she was the lead vocalist with the Cadets Showband and was very much in demand in the big ballrooms around the country. Although the big band scene has now ended, Eileen is kept busy singing in different venues and will be appearing in the Olympia during the Millennium Year in *Nunsense* with other popular artistes.

LUCY CHARLES FITZSIMMONS was born in Harcourt Street in 1912. She was an art student at the Metropolitan School of Art in Kildare Street and went abroad to study in Paris. She returned to Dublin when the Second World War started and was offered a job in the National College of Art. Later on she became Head of the College but retired from this position prior to its move to Thomas Street. She still continues to work at home as a portrait painter but no longer holds exhibitions.

CATHERINE DONNELLY was born in Dublin in 1948 and went to school in Mount Anvil. She later studied English in UCD and Law in the King's Inns. Her main interests are in the theatre and the cinema. She writes lighthearted feature articles for newspapers and also writes the advertisements for Ballygowan Spring Water, Power's Whiskey and Ryanair. At the moment she is a copy writer in McConnell's Advertising Service.

CLARE BOYLAN was born in 1948 and grew up in the Terenure area of Dublin. She has had a very successful writing career as both journalist and author. She was editor of two magazines *Young Woman* and *Image* and for many years worked with the *Evening Press*, first as a reporter, then as a writer of features, for which she received the Benson and Hedges award for outstanding journalism. She has written two books *Holy Pictures* and *Black Babies* and a book of short stories *A Nail on the Head*.

GERALDINE MURPHY devotes most of her spare time to voluntary work with the Westland Row Social Services Council and is on the Management Committee of CO-SEC, a Secretarial Co-op, which is based in the Tower at the IDA Centre in Pearse Street. Geraldine works as a Schools' Traffic Warden and is also a Peace Commissioner. Number 45 Eccles Street, where she lived as a child, has recently been demolished by the Mater Hospital, following which there was a public outcry because the house was officially listed for protection.

MAUREEN POTTER is a northside Dubliner who grew up on the stage in the 1930s. She is a much loved theatre personality who has played with all the great names, Jimmy O'Dea, Michael MacLiammoir, Hilton Edwards and Siobhan McKenna to name but a few. This year she has been honoured with the Freedom of the City and with a Doctorate from Trinity College. Her portrayal of Maisie Madigan in Sean O'Casey's *Juno and the Paycock* was much acclaimed and when the play goes to New York in June of this year, Maureen hopes to repeat her success in the part of one of O'Casey's famous characters.